SEX STEREOTYPES
AND READING:
RESEARCH AND STRATEGIES

Edited by E. Marcia Sheridan
Indiana University at South Bend
For the IRA Sex Stereotyping
and Reading Committee

International Reading Association
800 Barksdale Road   Newark, Delaware 19711

INTERNATIONAL READING ASSOCIATION

Copyright 1982 by the
International Reading Association, Inc.

Library of Congress Cataloging in Publication Data
Main entry under title:

Sex stereotypes and reading.

   Bibliography: p.
   1. Sex discrimination in education—Bibliography.
2. Sex differences in education—Bibliography.
3. Reading—Bibliography. I. Sheridan, E. Marcia.
II. IRA Sex Stereotyping and Reading Committee.
z5814.D5s49   [LC212]   016.4284   81-13699
ISBN 0-87207-732-2   AACR2

Contents

Foreword *v*
Preface *vii*

Contributors

John Downing
University of Victoria

H. Thompson Fillmer
University of Florida

Ramona S. Frasher
Georgia State University

Marguerite K. Gillis
Southwest Texas State University

Gloria R. Greenbaum
Augusta Country Day School
Martinez, Georgia

Talbot Hamlin
Allyn and Bacon

Nora Lee Hoover
Virginia Polytechnic Institute and State University

Carole Schulte Johnson
Washington State University

Richard May
University of Victoria

Lloyd Ollila
University of Victoria

Barbara Porro
University of Florida

E. Marcia Sheridan
Indiana University at South Bend

Foreword

One cannot live in the late twentieth century without realizing that the role of women has changed dramatically in many parts of the world. Economic necessity and the drive for equalization of opportunity on many fronts have brought this about.

It was inevitable that so fundamental a movement would have to be reflected in the education of children and particularly in the materials used in the schools for the teaching of reading.

This volume should be of assistance to all educators concerned with understanding and eliminating sex stereotyping in the materials and practices with which we help children and young people become efficient and discriminating readers.

Olive S. Niles, President
International Reading Association
1980-1981

Preface

During the past ten years there has been a great deal written about sex stereotypes in educational settings, instructional materials, trade books, standardized tests, and particularly reading materials. The International Reading Association established a committee to deal with sexism and reading in 1975. Professional organizations and publishers have published guidelines and resolutions related to sex stereotyping, and federal legislation covers sex discrimination in educational institutions. From what began as a consciousness raising experience has emerged as an area studied by professionals in a variety of academic areas and from many perspectives.

Perhaps beginning with the study of classroom reading textbooks, *Dick and Jane as Victims*, done by the National Organization of Women's Committee on Women on Words and Images in 1972, reading professionals have been concerned with sex role stereotypes. Various studies have investigated sex roles and reading including their affects on achievement, interest, and attitude. Other studies have examined changes in the content of reading materials related to the number of males and females as main characters, in pictures, and in career roles. Social justice through equal opportunity to experience oneself, regardless of sex, in a positive way in and through books is recognized as an inherent concern and value of reading educators.

The Sex Stereotyping and Reading Committee undertook a charge from IRA to develop this monograph intended for a wide audience. The purpose of this monograph is to reflect on the past decade to review what has been established through research, as well as to look at those practical strategies which have been effective in dealing with and eliminating sex stereotyping. The content of articles included is sufficiently theoretical and practical in nature that both researchers and classroom teachers will find something of value.

Part One includes articles which examine research on sex stereotypes and reading from sociocognitive, sociological, cultural, and value-oriented perspectives. The articles in Part Two examine reading texts and trade books from America's beginning to the present as well as consider the words used by and about males and females. Part Three presents three articles on strategies related to sex stereotypes and reading appropriate for classroom use. The appendix contains useful information for further study and use.

Many current and former members of the Sex Stereotypes and Reading Committee served as reviewers of submitted manuscripts: Carole S. Johnson, Ramona S. Frasher, H. Thompson Fillmer, Talbot Hamlin, Elizabeth H. Rowell, Ire A. Page, Melvin Graham, and Ann Bodkin. Special thanks is also given to Lloyd W. Kline and Fred Herschede for their support and advice and to Indiana University for awarding me a summer faculty fellowship enabling me to complete this monograph.

EMS

Part One
Cognitive, Social, and Educational

Sex Stereotypes in a Sociocognitive Model of Reading

E. Marcia Sheridan

The contents of school textbooks tend to be determined heavily by direct social pressures and by supply and demand. Within this context, reading educators have been drawn into discussion of a significant social issue regarding textbooks: Have instructional materials used to teach reading and literature in both elementary and secondary schools portrayed people primarily in traditional sex role stereotypes? If so, should instructional materials be changed to include representative numbers of characters in nontraditional sex roles? Or should we await evidence of *damage* from only traditional portrayals of male and female roles?

The purpose of this article is to present a model for examining the issue of sex stereotypes and reading from two basic viewpoints: the cognitive and the social or value-oriented. The research literature on concepts, cognitive structures, and theoretical models of reading will be reviewed in order to provide a framework for a sociocognitive view of reading and stereotypes. Recent criticism in the research literature regarding sex stereotypes and reading research will be examined from a social perspective.

A definition of a sex stereotype will be presented for the purpose of distinguishing the difference between traditional and nontraditional concepts of people in literature and also for making a distinction between stereotyped and nonstereotyped portrayals of people in reading materials. A position based on both conceptual clarity and social justice will be given to argue for the inclusion of both traditional and nontraditional people in reading materials as a value and ethical issue.

In May 1980, the International Reading Association adopted a resolution concerned with the availability of reading materials. This resolution acknowledged the existence of competing value systems in our society and opposed policies which excluded from all students certain materials for reading instruction (see appendix). When arguing for the inclusion of certain kinds of people in school literature, the issue of censorship often arises. The relationship between sex stereotypes and reading materials and the question of censorship will be examined in reference to the political value systems which propose or refute certain role model presentations.

Stereotypes as Concepts

Cognitively, what is a stereotype? By definition, a stereotype is a concept; a sex stereotype is a concept about men and women. There are several ways of acquiring and distinguishing among concepts. One way involves distinguishing concepts on the basis of critical or criterial attributes. This enables us to tell to which category an example belongs. For example, some rather obvious criterial attributes for distinguishing between men and women are differences in physiological characteristics.

Another way of describing the concept of a group of people is in terms of a prototypical model—the picture one has in one's mind that represents the model or ideal of the group (Lippman, 1951). On the basis of prototypical models and criterial physiological attributes, we might expect any given woman to be shorter than any given man, although we can easily recognize that there can be exceptions. Even if we happen to meet a very tall woman, we will probably maintain our perception of women as shorter because it is generally true; and the concept, while invalid in some instances, enables us to think in a form of mental shorthand.

Sheridan

Much of the work of school is teaching concepts. School reading materials constitute only one mode in which children acquire concepts about their cultural and sex roles in society. The family, religious training, peer group, and television are other modes of acquiring concepts of appropriate role behavior. Yet because the school plays such an important part of a child's life, the concept of males and females in school materials is a significant pedagogical issue. Evidence from recent studies indicates that while publishers have included more female main characters, parity between the sexes is far from a realized goal (Frasher, this volume; Britton and Lumpkin, 1977).

Cognitive Structures

How do children learn about male and female roles from the reading of literature? Piaget used the terms *assimilation* and *accommodation* to describe part of the learning process. As we integrate a new example into a preexisting concept, we are assimilating. When we have to change our concepts because they can no longer account for all the examples, we are involved in accommodation. For example, if our concepts of men and women include the idea that only men are doctors, then as long as we do not encounter a woman doctor we can assimilate new examples into the existing concept. But when we meet a woman doctor, we have to accommodate or change the concept in order to fit the new example. In other words, we learn that sex is not an absolute criterial attribute for being a doctor.

Ausubel (1968) adds some new perceptions to the way in which people learn. He describes the *ideational scaffolding* or cognitive structure which is made up of all the concepts in our mind. Many theoreticians view the mind in a concrete way, with ideational scaffolding giving an image much like a skeleton or framework for a building. Ausubel describes how what is already present in one's cognitive structure constitutes a filter, like a pair of eyeglasses through which we view the rest of the world.

Piaget's developmental model of learning describes stages in cognitive operations and functions. These stages include the sensorimotor period (0-2 years), the preoperational period (2-7 years), the concrete operational period (7-11 years), and the period of formal operations (11-15 years [Wadsworth, 1979]). New learning about people's roles is integrated or assimilated into one's preexisting cognitive structure.

Adding more flesh on the bones of ideational scaffolding is the more current concept in research literature—*schemata.* Schemata represent generic or superordinate concepts in one's cognitive structure, with a network of interrelationships among subschemata, subconcepts, or categories. In a sense, schemata represent stereotypes of concepts and knowledge rather than definitions. Schemata can be described at all levels of abstraction, can be embedded within one another in a hierarchical fashion, and can have variables or "slots" that are often filled by inference, usually on the basis of the most predictable or stereotypic representation (Rummelhart and Ortony, 1977).

There is a difference in connotation between using the word "stereotype" related to the acquisition of superordinate concepts and "sex stereotypes." Implicit in the meaning of sex stereotype is the understanding of *bias* which would include only partial evidence, be strong, rigid and would distort perception and other thinking activities. In a sense stereotypes, as well as prejudice, emotions, attitudes, and readiness, constitute the "materials of thinking" (Russell, 1956, p. 167).

To understand cognitive structure, consider the construction of a building. We start with the general shape or framework. This can be compared to the initial acquisition in childhood of concrete experiences. We gradually fill in particular rooms in the building; in Piagetian terms, we are assimilating as we acquire less idiosyncratic and subjective learning. As we refine our construction, we may change the size or location of a room or the shape of the building itself; this is analogous to Piaget's accommodation. Instead of assimilation and accommodation, one schema theorist uses the terms *schema usage* and *schema change,* but the meanings are similar (Anderson, 1977).

In assimilating new information, we attempt to identify its criterial attributes to determine whether it fits in one or another conceptual room or category. The rooms we already have in our cognitive structure or building cause us to be more or less aware of certain properties of the knowledge we view. Thus, our interpretation of what we are reading is influenced by the way we have organized what we have previously experienced and learned.

The constructivist view recognizes no objective view apart from our own interpretation believing "we see what we know" based on the construction, over time, of various versions or mental representations of the world (Gardner, 1980, p. 92). The relationship between the acquisition of concepts and sex stereotypes, cognitively, is much the same. There is a natural tendency to generalize or stereotype in order to facilitate storage and retrieval. Thus the nature of the input or material regarding people in reading is particularly sensitive.

The walls or criterial attributes of our concepts are not solid. Instead, the boundaries of our concepts are fuzzy, so concepts may overlap. We have to learn to tolerate the ambiguity of those fuzzy boundaries. Continuing our building analogy, we have to accept movable or wavy walls in our conceptual structure. In other words, we must keep an open mind. This is not only a moral judgment that the learner must make but is also consistent with further learning and a belief about the nature of knowledge—we haven't learned it all.

If we have little tolerance for ambiguity—if we have boundaries that are rigid and unyielding—our concepts and our misconceptions will be highly resistant to change. We will have closed our minds to new and perhaps critical information. Thus the child may continue to insist that all doctors are men even after encountering the woman doctor, elaborating the misconception of sex as a criterial attribute of the concept "doctor." Open-mindedness or tolerance for ambiguity is critical for new learning and is essential for all credible cognitive theories of learning and development.

The nature of representing males and females in literature and the language used to describe them can contribute to an elaboration of our concepts of sex roles or our misconceptions. Language itself is a reflection of culture, and it both reflects and determines "the mental operations (level of cognitive functioning) involved in the acquisition of abstract and higher order concepts" (Ausubel, 1978, p. 105). Language is also the way in which human beings communicate important aspects of the culture to one another.

The words we use represent generic concepts upon which there is a consensus of meaning. This is generally true except in relationship to generic words referring to males and females. Children do not readily understand that "he, his, man, men, and mankind," in the generic sense, also include "she, her, woman, women, and womenkind" (Fillmer, this volume). There is relatively more consensus on the meaning of concrete words than on those that deal with abstractions, such as sex stereotypes, for which various differences in connotation can arise. Two people with different dominant schemata might well define "masculine" or "feminine" to the point of an ideological stand-off. In such a case, one course of action is to simply accept that there is another point of view.

We learn language from first hand encounters, and the words we learn and the role models available to us vary with our own personal history and pattern of socialization. Words related to people are present in dominant schemata as *ideal types* or models with criterial attributes generalized to members of the group. By their very nature, ideal types tend to be one-sided and value-oriented. Particular ethnic, racial, and political groups may have different ideas regarding ideal types and models of people. Variations in experience and value systems account for how people infer and interpret differently from the same information (St. Clair, 1978).

In the field of social science, the construction of an ideal type is intended as a scientific tool, seeking perfection of a logical as opposed to moral or ethical model (Freund, 1969). The representation of role models or ideal types in school literature differs since the function of the school is to transmit the culture and the cognitive and social skills necessary in dealing with moral and ethical issues.

Conceptual Models and Theories of Reading

Just how does what the reader knows interact with what is

on the page to result in comprehension of the message? Elkind (1967) states:

> The silent reader gives meaning to the words he reads by relating these to the conceptual system he has constructed in the course of his development. The richness of meaning that he derives from his reading will depend both upon the quality of the material he is reading and upon the breadth and depth of his conceptual understanding (p. 337).

Communication between the reader and the writer is facilitated the more the reader's concepts are consistent with the concepts of his or her culture (Singer, 1976). Thus it is important that school texts reflect the multifaceted, multiethnic nature of American society, including both traditional and nontraditional roles of males and females.

As we read about people we are engaged in a cognitive process. Major areas of recent research on reading comprehension have used information processing models to describe the reading act, show how meaning is extracted or reconstructed from print, and illustrate the way in which information is shaped and stored from print by the reader. Goodman's psycholinguistic model (1976), Ruddell's communication model (1976), and Rumelhart's interactive model (1977) provide ways in which persons concerned with reading can conceptualize the way readers get meaning from print. LaBerge and Samuels (1976) propose a model which focuses on the way the reader processes features, letters, and spelling patterns into words that result in meaning. Goodman's model focuses on how the reader samples from the text, predicting meaning as opposed to processing feature by feature, letter by letter. LaBerge and Samuels' model is called a *bottom-up* model and Goodman's a *top-down* model of reading; the names emphasize the main focus of the level of processing. Rumelhart's model includes both levels of processing, stressing the simultaneous interaction of these levels from which an interpretation of meaning is derived.

The goal of *schema theory* is to describe the way information in a text is shaped and stored by the reader (Adams and Collins, 1977). The underlying assumption is that meaning does not lie solely in the print itself but results from an interaction between what is in the text and what is already in the reader's mind—the cognitive structure or schemata. These schemata represent the framework for understanding new information and constitute, in Smith's words, one's theory of the world in one's head (Smith, 1975). The schemata consist of what are variously called *concepts, prototypes, categories,* and *scripts,* which are cumulative, assimilative combinations of information about objects, people, events, actions, and sequences of action (Spiro, 1977). These constitute a cognitive filter through which one views the world and from which one predicts or makes inferences about what is read (Ausubel, 1968).

Brown has raised interesting questions regarding some of the current conceptual models and theories of reading. She has criticized developmental models of learning such as Piaget's stages of development for their inability to describe transformations as a result of growth and change. She points out that the schema theorists have left some significant questions unanswered. As more assimilative models, they neglect to explain how accommodation occurs, which could account for major shifts in perspective. How do transformations as a result of growth occur? Brown points out some flaws in the information processing models of learning as lacking "emotional factors such as attitudes, opinions, prejudices, fears of failure, etc., all important factors in determining the efficiency of any learning activity" (Brown, 1980, p. 13).

A Sociocognitive Model

The model in Table 1 provides a framework for conceptualizing social factors related to the role sex stereotypes play in reading and in the content of reading materials. What people read affects what concepts and stereotypes they have. There is an interaction between the psychology of learning and the social issue of the content of school materials.

Our schemata are formed in early childhood on the basis of concrete examples in our subjective experience. Inductively, children begin to identify the criteral attributes from a large number of examples to arrive at a concept. The particular nature of the schemata children construct is based on the experiences they have. Experiences are to a large extent determined by the

Table 1

A Sociocognitive Model

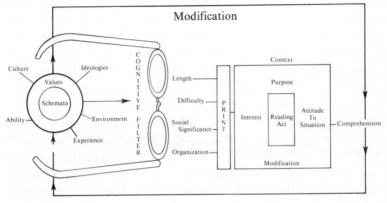

environment and culture in which children live and which present the examples.

It would be myopic to argue that if males and females were represented in equal proportions and in a variety of occupations in proportion to the racial and ethnic diversity of this country children's attitudes and values regarding sex roles would change. School learning is only one part of a child's life, and certainly more time is spent watching television than in reading books. Values about the roles of males and females may be resistant to change and, in respect to attitude change, Russell (1956) states that "attitudes may change if concepts or values change, and since values are resistant to change, attitude change depends largely upon change in concepts" (p. 17). At least in this sense, then, the portrayal of people in school reading materials presents a cognitive and a social issue of significance.

The particular political and economic ideologies to which the children are exposed, which they experience and learn from, and the ability of children to relate to a variety of similar examples, all contribute to concept and schema formation. As children develop, they assimilate new learning into preexisting schemata. Through the interaction of ability, experiences, environment, ideologies, culture, and a core of significant values, dominant schemata develop, constituting cognitive filters which shape the way children perceive the world around them as well as the way they interpret what they read.

Measurement and research on the comprehension of printed materials have frequently limited their concerns to the reading difficulty and organization of the text. Even more importantly, these materials have little social significance. Taken together, this means that these materials, in themselves, have little potential for a significant impact on the reader's dominant schemata related to social issues. Yet, one of the most significant aspects of reading is the potential of the material that one reads for changing one's view of the world. Think, for example, of the holy books of the world's great religions. Think of the writing of Darwin, Freud, and Marx, of Kant and Keynes. It is this potential for impact that causes groups and individuals to argue passionately for the inclusion or exclusion of particular works of particular ideas in instructional materials.

Most models of the reading process concern themselves primarily with the reading act itself. They are heavily "print bound." Too often, they omit or minimize the context in which the reader approaches and engages in the reading act. Factors such as readers' purposes for reading, and their motivations, interests in, and attitudes toward the material and the situation are not taken into account.

The sociocognitive model presents a framework for discussing not only characteristics of the text but also our schemata and the context of the situation. It demonstrates how our dominant schemata can modify our interpretation of what we read—and also how our interpretation can modify our schemata.

Sex Stereotypes as a Social Issue

How is stereotyping as a social issue affected by values regarding the appropriate roles of men and women? As we read about people in literature, we interpret and evaluate their actions not solely on the basis of the information presented by the author. Our inferences and evaluation of the people we read about are also strongly affected by our schemata for people, that is, our concept of what men and women are like.

Sheridan

The difficulty in dealing with "a concept for people" is that concept-symbols in general have what Ausubel (1968) calls "culturally standardized generic" meanings (p. 526). However, we are in a period in which concepts about men and women are not standardized throughout the culture, and in which there is a lack of consensus about the criterial attributes distinguishing masculine from feminine.

Our problem is complicated by the fact that we are dealing not strictly with definitions but with values. To a great extent, it is our values with respect to our schemata of ideal types of people that determine the way in which we interpret character actions in literature. The inclusion or exclusion of certain types of people in literature is, therefore, an issue of values.

A Concept of People

In processing the information we receive about people through the reading of literature, our fundamental concept of people takes on capital importance. The two predominant schemata for interpreting and evaluating people in literature can conveniently be referred to as *traditional* and *nontraditional*. A distinction also must be made between stereotypes and nonstereotypes.

Those who hold a traditional concept of males and females, and the values related to it, hold that there are at least three criterial attributes differentiating males from females: biological or genetic differences; a distinctive difference in their psychological makeup, which includes certain traits and qualities; and differences in the number and types of roles and activities in which they engage.

Those who maintain a nontraditional concept of people recognize that criterial attributes focus on both the differences and commonalities between males and females. One criterial attribute perceived in the nontraditional concept of people is in the biological or genetic category. There is an agreement in this category between both the traditional and nontraditional concepts of people, although there will probably be some disagreement over just what fits in the biological and genetic category as opposed to some other category, such as learned behavior. In the nontraditional concept of people, males and females are perceived as having much commonality with respect to the psychological qualities and traits and the number of types of roles in which they can engage. This does not mean that males and females are identical, simply that within these categories there are not mutually exclusive attributes based on sex.

Table 2

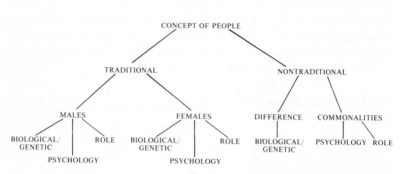

A sex stereotype can be defined as a concept about people that attributes to males and females mutually exclusive traits, has rigid or fixed boundaries, is applied to all members of the sex group, and is both evaluative and simplistic. By this definition, if instructional materials present *only* traditional images of people, they would have to be classified as stereotyped. By the same token, presenting *only* nontraditional images of people is also stereotyped.

Sex Stereotypes As a Value Issue

In a critical review of research on sex roles, Kingston and Lovelace (1977) raise issues that reflect value questions rather than questions which can be answered by research. After summarizing the research on occupational roles portrayed by women in various reading materials, they pose the question whether texts should portray a real or idealized view of women's roles or reflect the change in the roles of women. In fact, school readers in America have never portrayed the real world, but have in Hamlin's words (this volume) been "a selective reflector" of the world we want children to know and value. Another proposal in the Kingston and Lovelace paper is to delay any change in the portrayal of sex roles in textbooks until the issue of sex roles in reading materials has been "studied scientifically."

Tibbetts (1978) makes points similar to Kingston and Lovelace. She also calls for concrete evidence of damage from sexist content, again from the "scientific perspective." In promoting this empirical argument, critics such as these appear not to recognize that sexism and sex stereotyping in texts must be examined as much from a social and ethical point of view as from a scientific one. If the absence or distortion of minorities in textbooks is considered de facto to be racist, why must the absence or distortion of women in instructional materials await scientific verification before it is changed?

Kingston and Lovelace argue for "measureable, reliable, valid, and unemotional" definitions of "*sexist, sexism, bias, stereotyped,* and *degrading*" (p. 157). The nature of such words, however, makes it highly unlikely that everyone who uses them will agree on one definition. They are too much a reflection of one's values. Smith, Smith, and Mikulecky (1978) refer to words similar to these, such as *love, freedom* and *authority*, as having "nil formal definability" and of serving the particular purpose of the user or representing "one of several sets of values" (p. 201). They caution that the significance of such words must be considered in the particular contexts in which they are encountered.

As for waiting for evidence of damage, there are those who would argue that damage has already occurred. The same problem with respect to definition arises in the case of "damage" as it does in "sexist," "sex stereotype," etc. Even in the absence of evidence of damage, there have not been any good reasons proposed for not changing the content of reading materials to include nontraditional models of people.

If one role of the schools is the transmission of the cultural consensus of society, the question arises as to what the role of schooling should be in a period of social transformation where there is a lack of consensus, particularly with respect to the psychology and roles of males and females. The question is cognitive, ethical, and social. Most assuredly our points of view regarding the roles of men and women in textbooks reflect our values. At a minimum, even children whose parents want them to maintain a traditional concept of people should be aware that there are alternative ways of thinking and being.

Conclusion

The content of school readers is influenced by the prevailing social concerns which affect whether certain reading materials are bought or not. The 70s has been a period of concern over the portrayal of male and female sex role stereotypes resulting in changes in the content and illustrations of many reading programs. There is no doubt the content of reading materials in the early 70s was sexist (Women on Words and Images, 1972). Changes in many series occurred, some significant, others cosmetic (Britton and Lumpkin, 1977).

Because children learn from what they read, the content of reading materials and the nature of how children think about what they read have been both cognitive and social issues for reading teachers. The research on comprehension during the latter part of the 70s provided new insights into the nature of how children learn through reading. While it may be useful to have a preconceived idea or stereotype of "table" in our mind to facilitate thinking, a preconceived stereotyped notion of people inhibits thinking.

By presenting only persons in traditional roles in reading materials, we limit the role models to those acceptable to people who espouse a particular value system. In so doing, we contribute to children's misconceptions by presenting them with incomplete information regarding a concept of people. We limit them to only one point of view. In addition, by allowing such a practice to occur, we capitulate to the conservative censor who tends to allow the presentation only of a rigidly traditional model.

There have also been a number of articles in professional journals attacking studies on sex stereotyping and demanding evidence for harm done by stereotyping; demands are also made for a definition of stereotypes strict enough to make studies

Sheridan

replicable. Until damage can be proven, these studies suggest, textbooks should be left as they are. Such articles overlook the fact that sex stereotyping is a value issue and a social one, and that trying to eliminate stereotypes is a matter of ethics and research.

We are in a period of social transformation and evolution. We live in a country of cultural diversity with competing value systems. In a heavily financed and well-organized campaign, censors are objecting to student participation in any activities related to self-understanding, values clarification, personal and family emotional development, and introspective examination of social and cultural aspects of family life, including ethnic studies (Mikulecky, 1979). The censor calls for exclusion. The educator argues for inclusion. The censor calls for exclusive or nearly exclusive protrayal of traditional sex roles, the educator for a broadening to include a variety of roles and role models. The censor would narrow boys' and girls' choices—vocational, psychological, emotional, and others—to those traditionally associated with males and females; the educator would open any choice to any person. The difference is fundamental; it is one of values and ethics, and research.

References

Adams, M.J., and A. Collins. *A schema-theoretic view of reading comprehension.* Technical Report #32, Center for the Study of Reading, University of Illinois, 1977. ED 146 565.

Anderson, R.C. The notion of schemata and the educational enterprise: General discussion of the conference. In R.C. Anderson, R.J. Spiro, and W.E. Montague (Eds.), *Schooling and the acquisition of knowledge.* Hillsdale, New Jersey: Erlbaum, 1977, 415-430.

Ausubel, D.P. *Educational psychology: A cognitive view.* New York: Holt, Rinehart & Winston, 1968.

Ausubel, D.P., J.D. Novak, and H. Hanesian. *Educational psychology: A cognitive view,* Second edition. New York: Holt, Rinehart & Winston, 1978.

Britton, G., and M. Lumpkin. *A consumer's guide to sex, race, and career bias in public school textbooks.* Corvallis, Oregon: Britton, 1977.

Brown, A.L. *Learning and development: The problems of compatability, access, and induction.* Technical Report #165, Center for the Study of Reading, University of Illinois, 1980.

Elkind, D. Cognitive development and reading. In H. Singer and R. Ruddell (Eds.), *Theoretical models and processes of reading,* Second edition. Newark, Delaware: International Reading Association, 1976, 331-340.

Freund, J. *The sociology of Max Weber.* New York: Vintage Books, 1969.

Gardner, H. Gifted worldmakers, *Psychology Today*, September 1980, 92-96.

Goodman, K. Behind the eye: What happens in reading? In H. Singer and R. Ruddell (Eds.), *Theoretical models and processes of reading*, Second edition. Newark, Delaware: International Reading Association, 1976, 470-496.

Kingston, A., and T. Lovelace. Sexism and reading: A critical review of the literature, *Reading Research Quarterly*, 13, 1 (1977), 131-161.

LaBerge, D., and S.J. Samuels. Toward a theory of automatic information processing in reading. In H. Singer and R. Ruddell (Eds.), *Theoretical models and processes of reading,* Second edition. Newark, Delaware: International Reading Association, 1976, 548-579.

Lippman, W. *Public Opinion,* New York: Macmillan, 1951.

Mikulecky, L. Censorship and reading instruction, *Reading Teacher,* 33, 1 (October 1979), 4-6.

Ruddell, R. Psycholinguistic implications for a systems of communication model. In H. Singer and R. Ruddell (Eds.), *Theoretical models and processes of reading,* Second edition. Newark, Delaware: International Reading Association, 1976, 452-469.

Rumelhart, D., and A. Ortony. The representation of knowledge in memory. In R.C. Anderson, R.J. Spiro, and W.E. Montague (Eds.), *Schooling and the acquisition of knowledge.* Hillsdale, New Jersey: Erlbaum, 1977, 99-136.

Russell, D.H. *Children's thinking.* New York: Ginn, 1956.

Singer, H. Theoretical models of reading. In H. Singer and R. Ruddell (Eds.), *Theoretical models and processes of reading,* Second edition. Newark, Delaware: International Reading Association, 1976, 634-654.

Smith, C.B., S.L. Smith, and L. Mikulecky. *Teaching reading and secondary school content subjects.* New York: Holt, Rinehart & Winston, 1978.

Spiro, R.J. Remembering information from text: The "State of Schema" approach. In R.C. Anderson, R.J. Spiro, and W.E. Montague (Eds.), *Schooling and the acquisition of knowledge.* Hillsdale, New Jersey: Erlbaum, 1977, 137-166.

St. Clair, R.N. Sociolinguistics and reading comprehension, *Viewpoints in Teaching and Learning,* 54, 3 (July 1978), 35-42.

Tibbetts, S. Wanted: Data to prove that sexist reading material has an impact on the reader, *Reading Teacher,* 32, 2 (November 1978), 165-169.

Wadsworth, B.J. *Piaget's Theory of Cognitive Development,* Second edition. New York: Longman, 1979.

Women on Words and Images. *Dick and Jane as victims.* Princeton, New Jersey: 1972.

Sex Differences and Cultural Expectations in Reading

John Downing
Richard May
Lloyd Ollila

Introduction

We must begin with a note of caution. Theoretically based research on sex differences in reading is still in its infancy. Therefore, in this brief chapter, we cannot expect to arrive at any firm conclusions. Nonetheless, summarizing the current state of knowledge in the area may indicate trends and help delineate questions deserving further consideration.

We shall address three general questions regarding sex differences: Do such differences actually exist? How general are those differences that appear to exist? What are the causative factors leading to these differences? Because these questions are interrelated, we must discuss them together rather than as separate issues. Among causative factors, we shall discuss two obvious and very broad sets of explanations: heredity, or biologically-based causes, and environment, or culturally-based causes. When we find consistent differences between males and females under a wide variety of circumstances, we tend to interpret these differences as caused by some kind of biological difference. Many of us are guilty of the simplistic approach of treating as hereditary, differences that are widely found in specific cultures or similar cultures. Actually, behavioral differences which are found in several circumstances but not universally might be caused by both hereditary and environmental factors. It will take much more empirical research to be able to answer these questions. Thus, one problem facing those interested in reading and reading-related differences between males and females is the lack of reliable data from sufficiently varied contexts to sort out what the causative factors are and how they operate.

A Perplexing Welter of Research Findings

Much of the research evidence on differences between boys and girls in reading related behaviors comes from North America. These studies can be summarized as follows:

1. Most studies using reading readiness measures show significant differences in favor of girls over boys (Anderson, Hughes, and Dixon, 1957).
2. For children who are able to read, girls generally show superior attainment compared with boys in normal classroom situations in the primary grades (Dykstra and Tinney, 1969).
3. As North Americans grow older (age 6 to adult), reading related attitudes change and there is an increasing tendency to identify books and reading as female objects and activities (Downing et al., 1979).

Since it is quite common to find girls with above average readiness and achievement scores in samples from North America, it is tempting to generalize that this might be a universal phenomenon and, therefore, might be genetically based. Outside North America, however, the relationship between a person's sex and his or her reading readiness, achievement, and attitudes about reading are somewhat mixed. Contrary to findings in the United States and Canada, boys have been found to have superior reading achievement in Nigeria (Abiri, 1969), India (Oommen, 1973), Germany (Preston, 1962), and Finland (Viitaniemi, 1965). On the other hand, Malmquist (1958) indicates that Swedish girls are better readers than are boys. Mixed results have been reported in Britain (Morris, 1966; Kelmer-Pringle, Butler, and Davie, 1966), leading Downing (1980) to conclude that there is a weak trend for girls to achieve better than boys in reading, but "...the difference between the sexes is quite unimportant."

In examining the studies in various countries, it is obvious that few tests of reading achievement and few population samples are strictly comparable. Johnson (1973) reports that boys outnumber girls three to one in schools from which samples were drawn in Nigeria and, furthermore, attendance by girls is more irregular than by boys (Downing and Thackray, 1971). Thus, although results indicate a definite pattern in favor of boys, this does not necessarily demonstrate a reversal of female superiority in reading achievement since an argument could be made that girls in Nigeria do not have equal opportunities to learn to read as do girls in North America. Preston (1962) found boys in Germany superior to girls on reading tests. However, data analyzed by Thorndike (1973) from a different city at about the same time, showed that girls were slightly superior to boys (Klein, 1977). Klein (1979a), taking a closer look at Preston's findings, suggests that they are being used beyond their limitations. Klein also indicates that the content of the reading tests affects the scores attained by girls or boys. Dwyer (1976), in an analysis of test content, points out that females do better on tests of verbal ability, while males score better on vocabulary tests. Care must be taken to balance the test content in interest and form to avoid obscuring real sex related differences or similarities.

In terms of sex role attitudes people in Denmark and Japan, from elementary school through adulthood, tend to view books and reading as about equally appropriate for either sex. This may be contrasted with data from the United States, Canada, and England which favor reading as a female activity, at least for people of school age and older (Downing et al., 1979).

In large scale cross-national tests of reading carried out by the International Association for the Evaluation of Educational Achievement (IEA), no valid conclusions could be drawn regarding sex differences in reading across cultures due to serious methodological problems (Downing, 1973; Downing and Dalrymple-Alford, 1974-1975). Klein (1977) also reports a number of methodological problems with cross-cultural studies and with independent studies carried out in different countries. The rigor with which the data were collected and analyzed varies greatly from study to study.

Regardless of methodological flaws, reports from other cultures on sex differences in reading are sufficiently discrepant from North American findings to raise serious doubts that the "North American phenomenon" is universal. This variability of findings suggests that we look beyond genetic antecedents to cultural factors.

While sex differences in normal classroom reading and attitudes toward reading vary from country to country, sex differences in reading disabilities appear to be more consistent in the extant literature. Reports on reading disability for students in the United States (Crosby, 1969), Britain (Critchley, 1979) and Germany (Orlow, 1976) agree that boys are much more likely than girls to be referred to clinics as a result of reading problems. However, since most of the data on sex differences in reading disabilities come from clinic referrals, and such referrals are made for a variety of reasons, it is difficult to generalize from the results of these studies. An hypothesis involving genetic causation of differential reading disabilities could rely on the possible greater biological vulnerability of males to various ills (Eisenberg, 1966). Such an hypothesis could be used to explain several sex differences, including the greater incidence of boys who are classified as having developmental dyslexia.

Arguments for a maturational difference between sexes have been based on some evidence that girls begin to speak earlier than boys (Moore, 1967; Clark-Stewart, 1973). McCarthy, as early as 1935, reported that boys exhibited more language disorders and that there was a maturational differentiation between the sexes in verbal performance. According to Klein (1977), Maccoby and Jacklin feel it is probably true that the greater verbal ability of girls has a physiological basis. On the other hand, Dwyer (1973) states that, although such data can be accounted for by maturational explanations, the same data can be explained equally well by a combination of social and cultural factors.

There are at least two types of data that speak against a simple genetic hypothesis. One is the body of information documenting that, in some countries, boys show better reading achievement than girls. This suggests that, if there is a genetic superiority of girls, it can be outweighed by other factors. A second source of data comes from children who are not in the special group referred to clinics. For example, Gross (1978) randomly sampled 305 children from a population of 1,871 in kindergarten, second grade, and fifth grade in an Israeli kibbutz system. She found no significant differences between the sexes in either reading performance or in the incidence of reading disability cases. There may exist a genetic factor that makes boys more at risk than girls for reading disabilities, but, by itself, this is an inadequate explanation of the observed patterns of sex differences in reading achievement. In a review of many sex differences, Maccoby and Jacklin (1974) concluded: "There is so far little evidence for sex-linkage of any of the genetic determiners of other specific abilites such as mathematical or verbal ability" (p. 361). Fairweather (1976) drew a similar conclusion.

A more viable genetically related hypothesis stems from the often observed point that boys are more aggressive both verbally and physically (Maccoby and Jacklin, 1974, p. 352). Relating sex differences in aggressiveness to reading differences, Vernon (1957) suggested that perhaps the most likely explanation is that the reading disability in boys is often associated with emotional difficulties which are frequently aggressive. Thus, the boys are referred to clinics because these emotional difficulties, rather than reading disability, have brought them to the notice of teachers and parents.

It is also possible that girls' reading disabilities are being overlooked or are not being considered as urgent as are boys'. Klein (1977) reports that, out of 245 children in the Saskatoon Separate School System who were reading one or more years below grade level, 52 percent were boys and 48 percent were girls. However, over the years, boys have greatly outnumbered girls at a local summer reading clinic.

Two preliminary studies conducted by Blom, Frey, Prawat, and Jarvis (1980) lend support to the view that boys are oriented more toward a verbally receptive and motorically expressive mode of response. They suggest that this type of preference could place boys at a greater disadvantage when learning to read. Further studies need to be carried out to investigate whether early reading problems of boys may be based on an underlying language functioning *difference*, rather than a deficit. Blom et al. base some of their conclusions on the finding that poor male readers exhibited significantly more aggressive behavior than did good male readers and that poor female readers exhibited less aggression than did good female readers.

Somewhat analagous differences are found in data supporting the existence of sex-dependent sensory propensities. That is, children of a given sex may be more sensitive to information presented in a particular sense modality. Watson (1969) tested 14-week-old infants and found that girls learned under auditory reinforcement but not visual reinforcement, while boys learned under visual reinforcement but not auditory. The age of these children makes it difficult to account for differences in terms of cultural factors. An auditory male-female sensory difference has also been found for eight to ten year old children in a memory study involving free recall of nouns (May and Hutt, 1974). Girls performed better when the material was presented in the auditory mode, but little difference was found between the sexes when the stimulus words were presented in the visual mode.

Some Rival Cultural Hypotheses

In an attempt to establish some clear-cut hypotheses to investigate possible cultural causes of sex differences in reading achievement, both Dwyer (1973) and Downing (1980) have reviewed research and theoretical literature relative to three specific cutural factors that might explain sex differences in reading: bias in reader content, negative treatment of boys by female teachers, and cultural expectations of the male sex role.

The Biased Basal Reader Hypothesis

To assess the bias in basal reader hypothesis, Blom, Waite, and Zimet (1970) analyzed the content of over 1,300 stories in twelve of the most widely used basal readers in the United States. They found that these stories were of about equal interest to both boys and girls. For example, it was not true, as had been alleged, that the stories more frequently depicted feminine activities. Generally, in her review of the research literature, Dwyer (1973) could not find evidence of a biased basal reader effect that might account for sex differences in reading ability. Furthermore, Gibson and Levin (1975) state that evidence from cross-cultural studies suggests that "the relationship of reading content to reading achievement is not straightforward" (p. 534).

A recent study by Klein (1979b) examined the reading of 23 boys and 23 girls in grades five and six and found the majority of each sex benefited from reading sex-appropriate content and that the boys favored boy stories and the girls, girl stories. Klein questions, therefore, the effect on reading achievement if balanced content appears in the readers.

The Negative Treatment of Boys
by Female Teachers Hypothesis

The possible effect of a female teacher bias against boys has attracted fairly substantial attention. In part, this is because approximately 85 percent of elementary teachers in the United States are female, and the proportion is highest in the primary years when beginning reading instruction occurs. An example of this hypothesis is given by Fagot and Patterson (1969) who suggest that boys find it difficult to identify with female teachers and come to dislike school because of this conflict with their male sex role. If this hypothesis is correct, it would be expected that male teachers would be more successful in teaching boys to read than would female teachers.

A number of studies related to this hypothesis have yielded negative results with pupils in grade one (Cascario, 1972), grade four (Steele, 1967), grade five (Asher and Gottman, 1973), and grade six (Forslund and Hull, 1974). An especially interesting test of the teacher bias hypothesis was carried out by Preston (1979) in Germany where the majority of elementary teachers are male. He studied a sample of fourth grade classes in which all the children had had the same teacher for four years (since grade one). Preston concluded that the results "...do not support the hypothesis that boys' reading achievement is promoted by their having a male teacher or that girls' reading achievement is promoted by their having a female teacher" (p. 524). Forslund and Hull (1974) studied 47 male teachers and 47 female teachers and 2,672 grade six boys and girls and concluded that the sex of the teacher does not significantly affect the achievement of either sex at this level. In general, the fairly extensive research on this topic indicates that the sex of the teacher has little influence on the relative success of boys and girls in learning to read.

Another possible explanation for sex differences in reading achievement is that female teachers have difficulty relating to male pupils and perhaps are more punitive and critical toward them. However, the available data show that teachers behave similarly toward boys and girls during reading instruction (Davis and Slobodian, 1967; Good, Sikes, and Brophy, 1973). Although boys tended to interrupt the group more frequently than girls, teachers reacted no differently to boys than to girls when such interruptions occurred. Lahaderne (1976) reported that male and female teachers do not differ significantly in their treatment and perceptions of boys and girls, and suggested that perhaps social forces impinging on the school are more important. Asher (1977) summarized this research literature, stating that male and female teachers share common values about acceptable student behavior, behave similarly toward both sexes, and produce similar achievement with both boys and girls.

The Cultural Expectations of Sex Roles Hypothesis

The cultural expectations of sex roles hypothesis may be related to certain reported differences in the attentiveness and interests of boys and girls in reading activities.

Samuels and Turnure (1974) used a behavioral observation schedule to investigate sex differences in classroom attentiveness and its relation to reading achievement among a sample of American first grade children. They found that girls were significantly more attentive than boys during the reading period and concluded that "...the sex difference favoring girls frequently found in reading achievement seems to be mediated by an attentional variable" (p. 31).

Some evidence suggests that boys may pay less attention to reading unless it holds specific interest for them, thus overcoming the sex role conflict. Asher and Markell (1974) assessed individually the reading interests of children and found that the expected sex difference was exhibited in reading comprehension only with low interest material. Boys' and girls' performances were similar on high interest material, but with low interest subjects the boys appeared to be less motivated to perform well. Similarly, Braun (1969) studied the word retention rate of 240 kindergartners when words were interest loaded according to sex. He found that both word acquisition and retention were enhanced by the interest-loading, particularly for low ability children. Further, when McNeil (1964) and Atkinson (1968) used teaching machines to teach reading, the boys' scores showed greater improvement than the girls'. This led Dwyer (1974) to suggest that the appeal that the teaching machinery had for boys produced the increase in the boys' achievement. However, this question of interest and attention is a complex problem and the reader is referred to the Johnson and Greenbaum article in this monograph for a more thorough review of this topic before forming any general conclusion. Here, we will confine ourselves to relating boys' interest in and attentiveness to reading instruction to their possible perception of reading as a feminine activity.

The third hypothesis reviewed by Dwyer (1973) and Downing (1980) dealt with cultural expectations for the male sex role. Parents, teachers and other socializing agents can punish and reward children's behavior, contingent upon how they comply with culturally-determined beliefs and customs about how boys or girls should or should not behave. Dwyer (1974) suggests that North American boys are rewarded for participating in active, nonacademic activities. This role is, to a great extent, incompatible with good school achievement. Similarly, boys may be less likely to receive negative feedback for marginal or inadequate performance in reading. In terms of cultural expectations, if boys perceive reading as feminine, then this activity must receive less attention than activities perceived as more masculine. If parents, teachers, and peers agree with this expectation, they will accept or even encourage the more masculine activity since it reinforces their expectation. As pointed out by Maccoby and Jacklin (1974); "...if a generalization about a group of people is believed, whenever a member of that group behaves the expected way the observer notes it and his belief is confirmed and strenghtened; when a member of the group behaves in a way that is not consistent with the observer's expectations, the instance is likely to pass unnoticed, and the observer's generalized belief is protected from disconfirmation. We believe that this well-documented process occurs continually in relation to the expected and perceived behavior of males and females and results in the perpetuation of myths that would otherwise die out under the impact of negative evidence" (p. 355).

There are several sources of evidence that cultural expectations held by adults and older children may influence the development of sex role standards in younger members of the culture. Kagan (1964) found that second and third graders considered many school related objects and activities to be feminine. Consistent with this, Hill, Hubbs, and Verbal (1974) found that kindergarten boys thought that most school related objects were used by boys, but older children in grades two and four became progressively uncertain about sex related appropriateness of the same objects. With regard to reading in particular, Stein and Smithells (1969) found that the more popular belief of American children was that reading activities were feminine, and that older students (grade twelve) considered reading to be more feminine than did younger students (grades two and six). In this context, it is appropriate to note Maccoby and Jacklin's 1974 general statement that, "more social pressure against inappropriate sex typing is directed at boys than at girls" (p. 328). This suggests that boys have to be more wary of appearing feminine and, thus, will be more strongly affected by sex role cultural expectations.

Dwyer (1974) examined factors including IQ, sex role standards, and sex role preference among children seven to eighteen years old and concludes: "The results suggest that reading and arithmetic sex differences are more a function of the child's perception of these areas as sex appropriate than of the child's biological sex, individual preference for masculine or feminine sex role, or liking or disliking of reading or arithmetic" (p. 811).

Given that sex role stereotypes related to reading are to be found, one course of future research on the topic might be to look at the contribution of different causative agents. For example, how much of this bias is intentionally shaped by parents, teachers, and other socializing agents and how much is incidentally learned through mere exposure and imitation? There is a serious limitation to trying to answer such a question since we may be in the midst of a cultural shift. If the attitudes that are taught and imitated are changing, then the questions we ask may need to change also.

For example, we should not be too surprised if some of the findings reported on sex roles are not replicated in future investigations or cannot be repeated in particular communities. Over the past decade there has been a generally heightened sensitivity to the topic of sex role stereotypes. This factor is likely to contribute to a disparity between findings of future research projects and those already published. Indeed, as the incidence of sex role typing decreases, it may be increasingly difficult to isolate its cause.

One function that such research might serve is to define more clearly the present situation for a particular community, to see how much its attitudes have changed or how representative it is of the larger culture of which it is a part. Substantial deviation of a specific classroom, school, or community from larger segments of the population may call for an examination of the local situation.

Even if we can assume that a cultural shift regarding sex role typing has not progressed very far, a number of thorny problems still face us if we are going to meaningfully investigate possible causes. One consideration is that we are presently ignorant of the relationship between acquisition of the skill of reading and attitudes about reading. Are these two characteristics acquired simultaneously or in synchronous progression (Wohlwill, 1973)? That is, do children progress from both limited skill and partially formed attitudes to moderate skill and more clearcut attitudes and eventually to highly developed skill and firm attitudes? Or, alternatively, is there some sort of developmental priority in which one of the characteristics, perhaps attitudes, develops to a fairly sophisticated level before the other characteristic (skill) develops? Studies of the development of sex trait stereotypes among young children indicate that knowledge of such stereotypes increases between the ages of five and eleven, with more male traits than female traits being known at each age level. Cross-nationally, it has been found that a high degree of similarity exists in the nature of sex stereotypes being learned in the United States, England, and Ireland (Best et al., 1977). Data collected by May and Ollila (1980) indicate that Canadian preschoolers as a group do not have the same general cultural sex role stereotype regarding who reads and who uses books as do older Canadians. These data, when combined with those of Downing et al. (1979), show a shift from preschoolers' perceiving these factors as boy related, to elementary school children somewhat evenly divided on which sex is more associated with books and reading. This shift in attitude accelerates further between the elementary and secondary stages, with the latter being the time when it is likely for books and reading to be perceived as girl related objects and activities. These data are summarized in Table 1.

Table 1
Percentage of "Boy" Responses to Four Reading Related Items

	Preschool	Elementary	Secondary	Adults
Females	62.7 (67)*	43.6 (144)	30.0 (108)	30.3 (104)
Males	73.5 (69)	56.7 (138)	38.3 (77)	34.5 (97)

*Sample sizes in parentheses

Inspection of the table shows a clear-cut trend for both males and females to give fewer boy responses, and thus more girl responses, as years of schooling increase. The absolute level of boy responses is higher for male than for female responders at each stage of development but these differences are modest compared with the age related trends. [This combination of data is legitimate because May and Ollila (1980) and Downing et al. (1979) used the same test materials and similar populations].

The fact that this shift in attitude appears to occur at about the same time children begin formal schooling, which includes instruction in reading related skills, does not necessarily point to this instruction as causing the shift in attitude. There may be heightened sensitivity to the role that reading should have, and this can be communicated to the child via parents, teachers, and other socializing agents. Certainly, there is a pattern of awareness already at the preschool stage. May and Ollila (1980) obtained interview data from 64 Canadian preschoolers, with a mean age of 44 months, which showed that these children judged that fathers read more to boys than to girls and more to older children than to younger children. If this reflects the actual pattern of parenting, that could contribute to the development of sex role attitudes of the child as much as or more than other factors. While these interview data provide a clue to the greater incidence of reading being judged as a male activity among boys at the preschool stage, they are not compatible with the substantial age-related shift in both sexes to view reading as a female activity in later years.

It is interesting to note that, although there is an attitude shift toward regarding reading as a feminine activity from preschool to secondary school, results in Canada indicate that, while girls are superior in reading achievement early in elementary school, this pattern is sometimes reversed beginning about grade six (Klein, 1977). Fairweather (1976) states that the incidence of significant sex differences in reading achievement appears to decrease after age ten in the United States, also. Thus, in spite of the fact that reading is considered to be more girl-related, the girls in secondary school lose any significant superiority in reading achievement that they may have had in their earlier years at elementary school.

The role of reading attitude must be studied in greater detail, for, if adults consider reading more appropriate for girls, then teachers, both male and female, may be influenced in their expectations for the reading achievement of boys. This may contribute to the greater incidence of referral of boys to reading clinics. Palardy (1969) found that boys were less successful than girls in learning to read if they had teachers who believed that boys were not equal to girls in initial reading ability. "Teachers in our culture expect girls to excel in reading as compared to boys, and they do, at least until sixth grade..." (Gibson and Levin, 1975, p. 270).

The shift in attitude could reflect an initial basic sex difference in reading ability—the real superiority of girls in the initial learning act would perhaps indicate to boys that "reading is for girls." This could be strengthened in some cultures by the stereotype learned from older children and adults. In other countries it may perhaps be overcome by differing attitudes.

Future Research and its Practical Application

There are many other questions that need to be considered on this topic. For example, Klein (1977) proposed other questions that must be examined in greater detail, such as "Why is the initial headstart in reading demonstrated by girls in North America lost when adulthood is reached?" and "Why must the sexes be equal in reading ability or any other abilities, for example, mathematics?" (p. 885).

At this time, the hypothesis that culture is the main cause of sex differences in reading cannot be said to be conclusively or even adequately supported by findings in either cross-cultural or cross-national studies. The varied methodological procedures of independent studies preclude final conclusions, and the culture-dependent basis of tests makes it difficult to establish a single nonbiased measure of reading achievement cross-culturally.

To state that studies have not conclusively confirmed the cultural factor does not imply that a biological cause must be the explanation for differences in the reading achievements of boys and of girls in the elementary school years. The balanced view must be that it is not possible to completely rule out either one theory or the other.

Indeed, why should researchers continue to look for an either/or cause of sex differences? Reading is such a complex skill that both biological and cultural factors probably have an influence. Maccoby and Jacklin (1974) conclude that, where sex differences exist, the causes are probably complex and interactive. Although they rule out numerous myths of the physiological basis of sex differences in human behavior, they state that many of the findings are incomplete and inconsistent. Further studies will have to take into account not only the cultural and genetic factors but also the complexity of the reading act itself. It could be that component reading subskills are differentially influenced by genetic and cultural factors.

It should be kept in mind that, as with other sex related differences, the differences noted between sexes in reading are generally small in comparison to the range of differences within a sex, and have proved to be difficult to measure conclusively. Hubbard and Lowe (1979) caution that the tendency in such studies is to stress the differences more than the similarities. These authors suggest that both the effect of biology on behavior and the effects of behaviors and environments on human biology must be examined.

Research is just beginning to investigate these complicated questions. The first step in such investigation involves conducting extensive and rigorous studies using tests of reading and related skills that are truly comparable across languages and across cultures. In addition to cross-cultural studies, we need in-depth research within each single culture to investigate which sex related reading differences are consistent and valid in that particular culture. The quantity and complexity of research problems in studying the causes of sex differences in reading behavior and attitudes may seem daunting. But the reward will surely be worthwhile. For, when we know why boys and girls are different or similar in various aspects of their reading behavior, then we will be able to plan (with greater certainty of success) for all children to have their best opportunity to become fluent and habitual readers.

References

Abiri, J.O.O. World initial teaching alphabet versus traditional orthography. Doctoral dissertation, University of Ibadan, Nigeria, 1969.

Anderson, I.H., B.O. Hughes, and W.R. Dixon. The rate of reading development and its relation to age of learning to read, sex, and intelligence. *Journal of Educational Research, 50* (1957), 481-494.

Asher, S.R., and J. Gottman. Sex of teacher and student reading achievement. *Journal of Educational Psychology, 65* (1973), 168-173.

Asher, S.R., and R.A. Markell. Sex Differences in comprehension of high and low interest reading material. *Journal of Educational Psychology, 66* (1974), 680-687.

Atkinson, R.C. Computerized instruction and the learning process. *American Psychologist, 23* (1968), 225-239.

Best, D.L., and others. Development of sex-trait stereotypes among young children in the United States, England, and Ireland. *Child Development, 48* (1977), 1375-1384.

Blom, G.E., and others. Sex differences in receptive language and behavioral expression as they relate to early reading achievement. Paper presented at the meeting of the American Educational Research Association, 1980.

Braun, C. Interest-loading and modality effects on textual response acquisition. *Reading Research Quarterly, 4* (1969), 428-444.

Cascario, E.F. The male teacher and reading achievement of first grade boys and girls. Doctoral dissertation, Lehigh University, 1972.

Clarke-Stewart, K.A. Interactions between mothers and their young children: Characteristics and consequences. *Monographs of Society for Research in Child Development*, 1973, *38*, No. 153.

Critchley, M. *The dyslexic child.* London: Heinemann, 1970.

Crosby, R.M.N. *Reading and the dyslexic child.* London: Souvenir Press, 1969.

Davis, O.L., and J.J. Slobodian. Teacher behavior toward boys and girls during first grade reading instruction. *American Educational Research Journal, 4* (1967), 261-269.

Downing, J. *Comparative reading.* New York: Macmillan, 1973. Ann Arbor, Michigan: University Microfilms International, 1979.

Downing, J. Cultural expectations and sex differences in reading. In J.R. Edwards (Ed.), *Social psychology of reading.* Silver Spring, Maryland: Institute of Modern Languages, 1980.

Downing, J., and E.C. Dalrymple-Alford. A methodological critique of the 1973 IEA survey of reading comprehension education in fifteen countries. *Reading Research Quarterly, 10* (1974-1975), 212-227.

Downing, J., and others. A cross-national survey of cultural expectations and sex-role standards in reading. *Journal of Research in Reading, 2* (1979), 8-23.

Downing, J., and D. Thackray. *Reading readiness.* London: Hodder and Stoughton, 1977.

Dwyer, C.A. Sex differences in reading. *Review of Educational Research,* 43 (1973), 455-466.

Dwyer, C.A. Influences of children's sex role standards on reading and arithmetic achievement. *Journal of Educational Psychology, 66* (1974), 811-816.

Dwyer, C.A. Test content and sex differences in reading. *Reading Teacher, 29* (1976), 753-757.

Dykstra, R., and R. Tinney. Sex differences in reading readiness: first grade achievement and second grade achievement. In J.A. Figurel (Ed.), *Reading and realism.* Newark, Delaware: International Reading Association, 1969.

Eisenberg, L. The epidemiology of reading retardation and a program for preventative intervention. In J. Money (Ed.), *The disabled reader.* Baltimore, Maryland: Johns Hopkins Press, 1966.

Fagot, B.I., and G.R. Patterson. An invivo analysis of reinforcing contingencies for sex role behaviors in the preschool child. *Developmental Psychology, 1* (1969), 563-568.

Fairweather, H. Sex differences in cognition. *Cognition, 4* (1976), 231-280.

Forslund, M.A., and R.E. Hull. Teacher sex and achievement among elementary school pupils. *Education, 95* (1974), 87-89.

Gibson, E.J., and H. Levin. *The psychology of reading.* Cambridge, Massachusetts: MIT Press, 1975.

Good, T.L., J.N. Sikes, and J.E. Brophy. Effects of teacher sex and student sex on classroom interaction. *Journal of Educational Psychology, 65* (1973), 74-87.

Gross, A.D. Sex role standards and reading achievement: A study of an Israeli kibbutz system. *Reading Teacher, 32* (1978), 149-156.

Hill, C.E., M.A. Hubbs, and C. Verbule. A developmental analysis of the sex role identification of school related objects. *Journal of Educational Research, 67* (1974), 205-206.

Johnson, D.D. Sex differences in reading across cultures. *Reading Research Quarterly, 9 (1973-74),* 67-86.

Kagan, J. The child's sex role classification of school objects. *Child Development, 35* (1964), 1051-1056.

Kellmer-Pringle, M.L., N.R. Butler, and R. Davie. *11,000 seven year olds.* London: Longmans, 1966.

Klein H.A. Cross cultural studies: What do they tell about sex differences in reading? *Reading Teacher, 30* (1977), 880-886.

Klein, H.A. A closer look at cross cultural sex differences in reading. *Reading Teacher, 32* (1979a), 660-664.

Klein, H.A. What effect does non-sexist content have on the reading of boys and girls? *Reading Improvement, 16* (1979b), 134-138.

Lahaderne, H.M. Feminized schools: Unpromised myth to explain boys' reading problems. *Reading Teacher, 29* (1976), 776-786.

Maccoby, E.E., and C.N. Jacklin. *The psychology of sex differences.* Stanford, California: Stanford University Press, 1974.

Malmquist, E. *Factors related to reading disabilities in the first grade of the elementary school.* Stockholm: Almqvist and Wiksell, 1958.

May, R.B., and C. Hutt. Modality and sex differences in recall and recognition memory. *Child Development, 45* (1974), 228-231.

May, R.B., and L.O. Ollila. Sex role bias in the linguistic awareness of preschoolers, *Reading Research Quarterly, 16*, 583-595.

McNeil, J.D. Programmed instruction versus usual classroom procedures in teaching boys to read. *American Educational Research Journal, 1* (1964), 113-119.

Moore, T. Language and intelligence: A longitudinal study of the first eight years, Part 1. Patterns of development in boys and girls. *Human Development, 10* (1967), 88-106.

Morris, J.M. *Standards and progress in reading.* Slough, England: National Foundation for Educational Research, 1966.

Oommen, C. India. In J. Downing (Ed.), *Comparative reading.* New York: Macmillan, 1973. Ann Arbor, Michigan: University Microfilms International, 1979.

Orlow, M. Literacy training in West Germany and the United States. *Reading Teacher, 29* (1976), 460-467.

Palardy, J.M. What teachers believe—what children achieve. *Elementary School Journal, 69* (1969), 370-374.

Preston, R.C. Reading achievement of German and American children. *School and Society, 90* (1962), 350-354.

Preston, R.C. Reading achievement of German boys and girls related to sex of teacher. *Reading Teacher, 32* (1979), 521-526.

Samuels, S.J., and J.E. Turnure. Attention and reading achievement in first grade boys and girls. *Journal of Educational Psychology, 66* (1974), 29-32.

Stanchfield, J.M. *Sex differences in learning to read.* Bloomington, Indiana: Phi Delta Kappa, 1973.

Steele, J.D. *The relationship between teacher sex and the variables of reading achievement, sex role preference, and teacher-pupil identification in a sample of fourth grade boys.* Doctoral dissertation, Ohio University, 1967.

Stein, A.H., and J. Smithells. Age and sex difference in children's sex role standards about achievement. *Developmental Psychology, 1* (1969), 252-259.

Thorndike, R.L. *Reading comprehension education in fifteen countries.* Stockholm: Almqvist and Wiksell. New York: Wiley, 1973.

Vernon, M.D. *Backwardness in reading.* London: Cambridge University Press, 1957.

Viitaniemi, E. Differences in reading between the sexes, I-II. *Kasvatus Ja Koulu (Education and School), 51* (1965), 122-131, 173-180.

Wohlwill, J.F. *The study of behavioral development.* New York: Academic Press, 1973.

Girls' and Boys' Reading Interests:
A Review of the Research*

Carole Schulte Johnson
Gloria R. Greenbaum

For years the majority of trade books and stories in basal readers presented males as main characters and emphasized interests and activities traditionally associated with males. This had not been questioned because teachers and librarians were convinced that girls would read about boys but not vice versa. In the past decade, women have questioned many traditional theories and this belief has also come under scrutiny. Even if the belief were found to be true, i.e. that girls, faced with no alternative reading materials would read about boys, a concern regarding the educational effect of this unequal portrayal leads to an additional question. What is the long term consequence stemming from unequal portrayal of girls and women in terms of numbers, activities, and roles in these textbooks and tradebooks?

Many investigations of reading interests have been reported; over 300 studies were reviewed in 1960 (Gray) and the research has continued since then (Elliott and Steinkellner, 1979; Rougeau, 1978; Terry, 1972). Based on this research, there are several findings which previous reviewers of the research have generally accepted.

---

*The first section cites studies illustratively rather than extensively since there are so many studies on the topic of girls' and boys' reading interests.

1. Girls will read about boys and their activities (King, 1967; Norvell, 1958; Terman and Lima, 1925) but boys will not read about girls (Lazar, 1937; Lyness, 1951; Thorndike, 1941). Regarding this finding, it should be noted that while some of the recent studies confirm past research (Chiu, 1973; Elliott and Steinkellner, 1979; Feeley, 1974; Tibbetts, 1974) others report no sex difference in reading interests (Conway, 1975; Penney, 1973; Rougeau, 1978).
2. Sex differences in reading interests appear from age nine on (Harris, 1970; Norvell, 1958; Terman and Lima, 1931).
3. There have been fairly consistent findings regarding interests; boys prefer adventure, sports, science, and information while girls choose mystery, romance, home and school life, animals, and fairy tales (Norvell, 1958; Terman and Lima, 1925; Thorndike, 1941).

Although this research suggesting strong divergent interests of girls and boys at and beyond age nine has generally been accepted, it can be critiqued strongly with respect to its methodology and interpretation. In many studies children did not actually read the books; often they were reacting only to titles and annotations. The data collection procedures lack validity and reliability information; for example, checklists can be completed with little thought; answers may be given to please adults; listing books and reasons can be hindered by memory and ability to communicate; neither an expression of interest nor books checked out necessarily means material was read; and book records can be carelessly kept. Additionally, these studies lacked clear definitions and categories (Bleakley, 1977; King, 1967; Weintraub, 1969, 1977; Zimet, 1966).

Another concern about these studies is the emphasis which has been placed on the differences to the exclusion of the many similarities found between boys' and girls' interests. For example, some studies found areas of overlapping or similar interests rated somewhat differently; that is, boys' order of preference might have been adventure, sport, and mystery while girls' was mystery, romance, and adventure (Chiu, 1973; Thorndike, 1941; Wolfson, 1960).

A finding which often has been ignored is that within each sex a wide variety of interests has been found. Thus there is the danger of overgeneralizing the reading interest findings on the basis of sex, rather than looking at each reader and her/his unique interests (Asher, 1977; Lorocque, 1974; Moray, 1978). Past research appears to support the statement that girls will read about boys but boys will not read about girls. However, the findings, though consistent, are not strong evidence due to methodological problems and interpretations; researchers recognized the limitations and developed these research questions. How does interest affect the comprehension of girls and boys? Does interest depend on the sex of main character and/or the story content? Are there educational effects due to the use of traditional or nontraditional materials?

Interest and Comprehension

Research has indicated fairly consistently that when given a choice, girls and boys both prefer to read about a same-sex main character. Since boys received the largest percentage of special reading help, it seemed sensble to ask whether boys' comprehension was affected by interest to a greater extent than girls' comprehension. A 1955 study (Bernstein) reported that boys showed a marked increase in comprehension on high interest material while girls did not (no significance was stated). Then in 1974 a study in which reading materials were chosen on the basis of individual students' measured interests found that, although girls and boys comprehended high interest material equally well, boys comprehended significantly less well on low interest material (Asher and Markell). A 1976 study found a nonsignificant trend that high interest increased the instructional level of informal reading inventories for boys more than for girls (Walker). Another study used a cued-choice condition (for reading, students chose five passages on the basis of 25 general topics such as sports or animals), a blind-choice condition (students chose five from blank folder covers) and a no-choice condition (students were given five passages to read). Boys but not girls significantly improved their comprehension in the cued-choice (knowledgeable choice) condition (Bowermaster, 1976).

Only boys were used in a study that found no relationship between interest and comprehension (Brooks, 1971). Six additional studies found that girls and boys did not differ significantly in their relationship between interest and comprehension (Asher, 1975; Asher, Hymel, and Wigfield, 1978; Henry, 1969; Koch, 1974; Saoi, 1976; Schickedanz, 1973).

In summary, four studies using fifth through ninth graders lend some support to the claim that interest affects boys' comprehension to a greater extent than it does girls' comprehension. A variety of interest measures were used with only one study using individual measures of interest, so perhaps interest was not truly involved. Two studies used cloze and one used multiple choice and free response as measures of comprehension. Basically, support for the claim is not strong; two studies clearly found significance while another did not report whether the results were significant; one found only a trend and the last found significance but since it was in a cued-choice format it is possible that knowledgeable choice rather than or combined with interest was operative.

Seven studies do not support the claim. Generally, subjects were fourth through sixth graders, though one study used third graders. Four of these seven studies did use individually identified interest materials. Five studies used the cloze, one used multiple choice, and one used both the cloze and multiple choice comprehension measures. All of these studies clearly found that interest affected comprehension similarly for both sexes. At this time the weight of the research does not substantiate the claim that interest has a greater effect on boys' comprehension than on girls'.

Sex of Character/Story Content

One striking aspect of the studies of the relationship of protagonist and story content to interest and/or comprehension is their recency. No study found was reported before 1970.

Investigating the effect of sex of main character was done in four studies. "Pippi Longstocking" was read to third graders. The study found that both sexes chose Pippi as their favorite character by wide margins. Interpretation of the total data led the author to conclude that boys did not reject a character solely on the basis of sex, but that content, personality, and behavior played equal, if not greater, roles (Frasher, 1977).

Eight story segments were read by fourth through sixth graders. No significant difference was found in story preference on the basis of sex of character. The author suggested that this finding supported the idea that content might affect interest (Lovelace, 1980).

Third and fourth graders read a series of stories in which all main characters participated in traditional masculine activities. Three story conditions were used: 1) the majority of main characters were female, 2) the majority of main characters were male, or 3) the main characters were equally male and female. They found that story evaluations did not vary as a function of sex of main character. This finding supports the idea that content rather than sex of main character is an important variable (Scott and Feldman-Summers, 1979).

Second, fifth, and seventh graders each read six books with females and six with males as protagonists. The books were chosen on the basis of appropriateness for grade level, literary quality, and androgynous main character, defined as a blending of positive female and male personality traits and behaviors. There were no significant differences in girls' and boys' ratings of books with male main characters (supporting idea that both girls and boys will read about boys). The findings of no signficant difference of boys' ratings of books with female or male main characters and comments obtained during interviews support the position that for boys it is the content or activities, not the sex of character, which is important. Second and seventh grade girls rated books with female main characters significantly higher than those with male main characters; the reverse was true for fifth grade girls. This "roller coaster" effect was explained on the basis of psychosexual development. The three conclusions were that responses to books are not determined by a relationship between sex of reader and sex of protagonist; androgynous characteristics do minimize the influence of the character's sex on response; and that the psychosexual development appears to influence a reader's response (Coley, 1980).

The effect of story content was investigated in three studies. In the first study only female characters were used. Seventh and eighth graders listened to five paired stories where the character was either aggressive or passive and five paired stories about female or male occupations. Girls' and boys' story preferences were significantly different in only two of ten choices (20 percent); boys significantly preferred only two stories, both with nontraditional characters; girls had no significant preference for female or male occupations; their significant choices on personality favored both aggressive and passive characters in separate stories (Rakes, Bowman, and Gottfred, 1977).

Nine to twelve year olds read traditional and nontraditional stories. Girls significantly preferred both the nontraditional story and main character while boys did not have a significant preference for either. The authors concluded that a reader's sex could not be assumed to determine interest or preference (Frasher and Frasher, 1978).

Black high school students read 44 brief story summaries, covering 11 plot categories. A significant sex of reader by category interaction was found which indicated that girls and boys react differently to some content; for example, female interests were more clearly defined than male interests and females were highly interested in all romance stories (the race of the characters did not matter) while males were interested in only the black/white romance stories (Katz, 1979).

Three investigators studied the effect of both sex of protagonist and story content. The earliest study had fifth graders respond to female and male versions about a ballet dancer and a pilot. No significant difference on the cloze comprehension score for female or male versions was found for either girls or boys (Klein, 1970).

Tenth through twelfth graders responded to 32 story summaries. Sex of protagonist tended to influence interest, but less so for girls; setting was significant for determining the interest of boys; and both sexes liked an action style, but girls equally liked an introspective style (Yoder, 1977).

In a variation of Klein's 1970 study, Metz (1978) had fifth graders read two stories, one female and one male in the same occupation, either pilot or dancer. This study, like Klein's, found that sex of character did not significantly influence comprehension for either girls or boys. Metz's study, going beyond Klein's, also found that the boys preferred a "masculine" role but either sex could portray it, while girls preferred either sex in a "feminine" role or a female in a "masculine" role. The pilot was equally interesting to both sexes. The author concluded that charcter role was more important than character sex for interest, and that the exclusion of nonstereotyped sex roles was detrimental to girls' interests but their inclusion was not detrimental to boys' interests.

None of these studies support the idea that sex of protagonist is of utmost importance for boys; in fact, the research would tend to indicate there might be a stronger relationship for girls than for boys. Some studies find a same sex preference, but it is not a consistent finding. More important, sex of character does not appear to influence comprehension. The studies that investigated content, including the two using comments from children, strongly indicate that content is of greater importance than sex of character in children's response to stories.

Traditional/Nontraditional Materials

Studies investigating the effects of various materials on girls and on boys were classified into two categories: effects of sex biased materials and effects of traditional/nontraditional activities. Studies using career guidance materials were not included.

Five studies and one review were found that investigated the effect of sex biased materials. One study found a significant effect on one of three learning measures, retention; girls and boys both retained the same sex interest words better, though the finding for girls was not clear due to a significant three-way interaction (Braun, 1969). A study of critical thinking skills found a significant test by sex interaction suggesting that performance was based on the sex interest of the material (Brown and Cook, 1975).

College students performed significantly better on test items containing references to their own sex, though there was some indication this might be due to item content rather than sex referents (Brown, 1975). Another study found no significant difference on tests due to same sex referent passages and items. Since a trend was found in the expected direction, the authors felt that cumulative scores or disproportionate sex referent items could magnify the differences (Moss and Brown, 1979).

A passage about the thinking patterns of children was read by college students. The sex of the child used in the passage was varied, either generic (abstract collective figures) or specifically named individuals. The results indicated that sex was attributed on the basis of the gender of the pronouns used (Buchanan, 1976). One review of six additional studies of generic usage reported that all studies agreed that when traditional generic pronouns and/or nouns were used, the antecedents were more likely to be interpreted as male (Johnson, 1977).

Eleven studies involved actual reading materials. Three studies used girl and boy content as their focus. One found no significant difference on the recall test for any type of girl-boy content; however, a significant difference between the sexes on the critical reading test indicated both were affected by the sex orientation of the material (Groff, 1967). Another reported that boys' comprehension did not depend on content but girls' did (Klein, 1970). In the last study, comprehension of the male stories did not differ but the girls' comprehension of female stories was significantly higher than the boys'. The author suggested that girls might be penalized by not having their interests met (Klein, 1979).

The results of a second group of three studies possibly could be explained on the basis of uniqueness of the content. One study of preschoolers found a higher recognition of nontraditional roles than of traditional ones (Kummerow, 1974) while another found that although girls and boys significantly preferred the character in the traditional role, they recalled significantly more about the nontraditional character (Jennings, 1975). Nine to twelve year olds read traditional and nontraditional stories, with sex of the main character being the same as the reader's. Neither sex had greater comprehension or preference for the traditional story about their own sex. Both had

Johnson and Greenbaum

significantly higher comprehension of the nontraditional story which the girls also significantly preferred. The boys did not have a significant story preference (Frasher and Frasher, 1978).

Two studies were found which showed behavioral changes. After being given a choice of toys, preschoolers were read either a stereotyped or nonstereotyped story. Then they chose from the same toys again. Those who heard a stereotyped story chose a stereotyped toy significantly more often, while those hearing a nonstereotyped story significantly more often chose a nonstereotyped toy (Ashton, 1978). A significant story by condition interaction was reported in the other study. All stories read used traditional male activities but in the female dominant condition the majority of main characters were female while in the male dominant condition they were male. It was found that both girls' and boys' perceptions of the numbers of girls who could engage in the activity read about was increased significantly in the female majority condition (Scott and Feldman-Summers, 1979).

A final group of four studies was concerned with the effect of sex of main character on comprehension. In one, neither sex had a significant difference in comprehension on the basis of sex of main character (Klein, 1970). After a story was read by college students, the amount recalled did not depend upon the sex of the main character (Buchanan, 1976). In a study of three story types (humor, mystery, and adventure), no significant difference in comprehension was found on the basis of sex of main character, even though both girls and boys significantly preferred the character of the same sex (Bleakley, 1977). The last investigation used three groups: one group read two stories with the main character of the same sex as the reader but one traditional theme and the other a nontraditional theme; another read two stories with the main character of the opposite sex of the reader and again traditional and nontraditional story themes were used; the final group read all four stories. Girls and boys significantly preferred the same sex main character; however, boys who read all four stories did have significantly better comprehension with male rather than female main characters.

Sex of character did not affect girls' comprehension while traditional/nontraditional themes did not affect comprehension for either sex (Frasher and Frasher, 1979).

In summarizing these studies, it can be said that 1) sex bias in educational material can have an effect; 2) girl and boy interest does appear to have some effect though Klein (1979) noted that 30 percent of each sex had a higher comprehension score on the opposite sex content; 3) it would appear that nonstereotyped behavior can be encouraged through nonstereotyped books; and 4) this review of studies of traditional/nontraditional materials and stories, while not proof of harm, definitely established a research basis for concern about the effect of sex biased educational curricula.

On the basis of this review of the literature, the following conclusions can be made:

1. The voluminous studies which found interest differences based on sex can be criticized on the basis of data collection procedures and instruments used.
2. Girls will read about boys and their activities but that says nothing about girls' preferences or the possible limiting effects of using such materials.
3. Boys will read about girls, it is not the sex of the protagonist that is important to boys but the story content. Boys tend to reject both female and male characters when the content is not appealing to them.
4. Girls and boys have many overlapping reading interests, although girls tend to have a wider variety of interests.
5. Research to date does not support the belief that interest has a greater effect on boys' comprehension than on girls'. Thus the traditional basis for the unequal representation of males in educational reading materials is not supported by the research.
6. The research discussed regarding the use of sex biased and/or traditional/nontraditional materials is not definitive in terms of their educational effects. However, results suggest that educators should be concerned because of possible educationally harmful effects.

7. The use of nontraditional material apparently contributes to a wider view of appropriate roles and behaviors.

8. One of the most important educational implications of this review is that, in terms of interest and learning, we must remember the uniqueness of the individual student. After all, Klein (1979) found that 30 percent of both girls and boys learned more from "cross-sex" material.

Together, these findings suggest the following generalization: We need not concern ourselves with sex interests in reading, but we do need to be concerned with the individual's interests. Overall, research supports the inclusion of women and men, girls and boys in educational materials, portrayed in a wide variety of roles and activities, both traditional and nontraditional. It is neither accurate nor fair to the individual to make educational decisions regarding reading interests and learning solely on the basis of sex.

References

Asher, Steven R. *Effect of interest in material on sex differences in reading comprehension.* Champaign, Illinois: University of Illinois, 1975. ED 109 610

Asher, Steven R. *Sex differences in reading achievement. Reading Education Report No. 2.* Champaign, Illinois: University of Illinois at Urbana-Champaign, 1977. ED 146 567

Asher, Steven R., and Richard A. Markell. Sex differences in comprehension of high and low interest reading material. *Journal of Educational Psychology,* 66 (October 1974), 680-687.

Asher, Steven R., Shelley Hymel, and Allan Wigfield. Influence of topic interest on children's reading comprehension. *Journal of Reading Behavior,* 10 (Spring 1978), 35-47.

Ashton, Eleanor. The effect of sex role stereotyped picture books on the play behavior of three and four year old children. Doctoral dissertation, University of Massachusetts, 1978. *Dissertation Abstracts International,* 39 (1978), 1310A. University Microfilm No. 7816228

Bernstein, Margery R. The relationship between interest and reading comprehension. *Journal of Educational Research,* 49 (December 1955), 283-288.

Bleakley, Mary Ellen. The effect of the sex of the main character in selected mystery, humor, and adventure stories on the interest and comprehension of fifth grade children. Doctoral dissertation, University of Colorado at Boulder, 1977. *Dissertation Abstracts International,* 38 (1977), 2542A. University Microfilm No. 7724188

Bowermaster, Janet Marie. *The effects of choice on children's reading comprehension and attitudes.* Champaign, Illinois: University of Illinois at Urbana-Champaign, 1976. ED 117 684

Braun, Carl. Interest-loading and modality effects on textual response acquisition. *Reading Research Quarterly,* 4 (Spring 1969), 428-444.

Brooks, Ruth Ann. An investigation of the relationship between reading interest and comprehension. Doctoral dissertation, The Ohio State University, 1971. *Dissertation Abstracts International,* 32 (1972), 6674A. University Microfilm No. 7215177.

Brown, Frederick G. Sex biases in achievement test stems: Do they have any effect on performance? Unpublished manuscript, Iowa State University, 1975.

Brown, Lester E., and Ellen Cook. How children's interests affect their critical thinking ability. *Educational Leadership,* 32 (February 1975), 339-342.

Buchanan, Lillian. The gender of generic pronouns and its effects on identification and memory. Doctoral dissertation, Kent State University, 1976. *Dissertation Abstracts International,* 38 (1977), 6359A. University Microfilm No. 777813

Chiu, Lian-Hwang. Reading preferences of fourth grade children related to sex and reading ability. *Journal of Educational Research,* 66 (April 1973), 369-373.

Coley, Carroll Brundage. Reader response to androgynous characterization in juvenile fiction at second, fifth, and seventh grade levels. Doctoral dissertation, Washington State University, 1980.

Conway, Hannah Elizabeth Miller. Reading interests of children in grades four through eight. Doctoral dissertation, The University of Alabama, 1975. *Dissertation Abstracts International,* 36 (1976), 5800A-5801A. University Microfilm No. 764801

Elliott, Peggy Gordon, and Lesley Linde Steinkellner. Reading preferences of urban and suburban secondary students: Topics and media. *Journal of Reading,* 23 (November 1979), 121-125.

Feeley, Joan T. Interest patterns and media preferences of middle-grade children. *Elementary English,* 51 (October 1974), 1006-1008.

Frasher, Ramona S. Boys, girls, and Pippi Longstocking. *Reading Teacher,* 30 (May 1977), 860-863.

Frasher, Ramona S., and James M. Frasher. Influence of story characters' roles on comprehension. *Reading Teacher,* 31 (November 1978), 160-164.

Frasher, Ramona, and James M. Frasher. *Gender roles in children's stories: Effects on preference and comprehension.* Atlanta: Georgia State University, 1979. ED 171 384

Gray, William S. Reading: Physiology and psychology of reading. In Chester W. Harris (Ed.), *Encyclopedia of educational research,* Third Edition. New York: Macmillan, 1960.

Groff, Patrick J. Children's attitudes toward reading and their critical reading abilities in four content-type materials. In Martha L. King, Bernice D. Ellinger, and Willavene Wolf (Eds.), *Critical reading.* New York: J.B. Lippincott, 1967.

Harris, Albert J. *How to increase reading ability.* New York: David McKay, 1970.

Henry, Peggy Elaine. The effect of interest on reading comprehension as measured by cloze and multiple choice tests. Doctoral dissertation, The University of Iowa, 1969. *Dissertation Abstracts,* 30 (1970), 3857A. University Microfilm No. 704369

Jennings, S.A. Effects of sex typing in children's stories on preference and recall. *Child Development,* 46 (1975), 220-223.

Johnson, Carole Schulte. Sexism in language: The case for including everybody. *Sex role stereotyping in the schools,* Revised Edition. Washington, D.C.: National Education Association, 1977, 1-8.

Katz, Rita Shirley. Reading interests responses of black adolescents to a biracial annotated fictitious titles survey. Doctoral dissertation, University of Pittsburgh, 1979. *Dissertation Abstracts International,* 40 (1979), 2448A-2449A. University Microfilm No. 7924724

King, Ethel M. Critical appraisal of research on children's reading interests, preferences, and habits. *Canadian Education and Research Digest,* 7 (December 1967), 312-326.

Klein, Howard A. Interest and comprehension in sex typed materials. In Jane H. Catterson (Ed.), *Children and Literature.* Newark, Delaware: International Reading Association, 1970.

Klein, Howard A. What effect does nonsexist content have on the reading of boys and girls? *Reading Improvement,* 16 (Summer 1979), 134-138.

Koch, Robert Emil. Relationship between reading interests and reading comprehension among fourth grade and sixth grade students. Doctoral dissertation, University of Illinois at Urbana-Champaign, 1974. *Dissertation Abstracts International,* 36 (1975), 7126A-7127A. University Microfilm No. 7511661

Kummerow, Kay Louise. *The relationship of age and sex of four, five, and six year olds to the perceptions of sex roles as portrayed in children's literature.* Tallahassee: Florida State University, 1974. ED 097 124

Larocque, Geraldine E. Adolescent literature: The student voice. *Journal of Reading,* 18 (December 1974), 219-224.

Lazar, May. *Reading interests, activities, and opportunities of bright, average, and dull children.* New York: Bureau of Publications, Teachers College, Columbia University, 1937.

Lovelace, Terry. Elementary readers' inferences and preferences for characteristics of protagonists in stories. In M.L. Kamil and A.J. Moe (Eds.), *Reading research: Studies and applications,* 1979, 249-253.

Lyness, Paul I. Patterns in mass communications taste of the young audience. *Journal of Educational Psychology,* 42 (December 1951), 449-467.

Metz, Susan Ellen Shapiro. *Sex roles in reading materials: Effects on children's reading comprehension and interest.* New Brunswick: Rutgers, The State University of New Jersey, 1978. ED 149 299

Moray, Geraldine. What does research say about the reading interests of children in the intermediate grades? *Reading Teacher,* 31 (April 1978), 763-768.

Moss, Jacques D., and F.G. Brown. Sex bias and academic performance: An empirical study. *Journal of Educational Measurement,* 16 (Fall 1979), 197-201.

Norvell, George W. *What boys and girls like to read.* Morristown, New Jersey: Silver Burdett, 1958.

Penney, Mary Elizabeth. Televiewing interests and reading interests of seventh grade students of Shawnee, Oklahoma. Doctoral dissertation, The University of Oklahoma, 1973. *Dissertation Abstracts International,* 34 (1973), 6598A. University Microfilm No. 7315331

Rakes, Thomas A., Harry L. Bowman, and Sandra Gottfred. Reader preference as related to female aggressiveness and stereotyped character roles. *Reading Improvement,* 14 (Spring 1977), 30-35.

Rougeau, Bernice Bourque. The interests of elementary school children as revealed through the individual interview technique. Doctoral dissertation, The University of Alabama, 1978. *Dissertation Abstracts International,* 39 (1978), 2053A-2054A. University Microfilm No. 7819213

Saoi, Arlys L. The effects of levels of interest, achievement, and self-concept on the reading comprehension scores of fourth grade boys and girls. Doctoral dissertation, University of South Dakota, 1976. *Dissertation Abstracts International,* 38 (1977), 6378A. University Microfilm No. 773454

Schickedanz, Judith Ann. The relationship of sex typing of reading to reading achievement and reading choice behavior in elementary school boys. Doctoral dissertation, University of Illinois at Urbana-Champaign, 1973. *Dissertation Abstracts International,* 35 (1974), 7645A. University Microfilm No. 7412176

Scott, Kathryn P., and Shirley Feldman-Summers. Children's reactions to textbook stories in which females are portrayed in traditionally male roles. *Journal of Educational Psychology,* 71 (June 1979), 396-402.

Terman, Lewis M., and Margaret Lima. *Children's reading.* New York: Appleton-Century-Crofts, 1925.

Terman, Lewis M., and Margaret Lima. *Children's reading: A guide for parents and teachers.* New York: Appleton-Century-Crofts, 1931.

Terry, Carolyn Ann. A national survey of children's poetry preferences in the fourth, fifth, and sixth grades. Doctoral dissertation, The Ohio State University, 1972. *Dissertation Abstracts International*, 33 (1972), 3973A-3974A. University Microfilm No. 732144

Thorndike, Robert L. *Children's reading interests.* New York: Bureau of Publications, Teachers College, Columbia University, 1941.

Tibbetts, Sylvia-Lee. Sex differences in children's reading preferences. *Reading Teacher*, 28 (December 1974), 279-281.

Walker, Martha Susan Motley. The effect of high and low interest content on instructional levels in informal reading inventories. Doctoral dissertation, Auburn University, 1976. *Dissertation Abstracts International*, 37 (1976), 2623A. University Microfilm No. 7625694

Weintraub, Samuel. Research: Children's reading interests. *Reading Teacher*, 22 (April 1969), 655-659.

Weintraub, Samuel. Two significant trends in reading research. In H. Alan Robinson (Ed.), *Reading and writing instruction in the United States: Historical trends.* Newark, Delaware: International Reading Association and Eric Clearinghouse on Reading and Communication Skills, 1977.

Wolfson, Bernice J. What do children say their reading interests are? *Reading Teacher*, 14 (November 1960), 81-82, 111.

Yoder, Janice Miller. The relative importance of four narrative factors in the reading interests of male and female adolescents in grades ten through twelve. Doctoral dissertation, The University of Iowa, 1977. *Dissertation Abstracts International*, 39 (1978), 217A. University Microfilm No. 7810400

Zimet, Sara F. Children's interest and story preferences: A critical review of the literature. *Elementary School Journal*, 67 (December 1966), 122-130.

Part Two
Reading, Writing, and Language

American Reading Materials: A Selective Reflector
Talbot Hamlin

In the 1960s and 1970s, the attention of educators was increasingly called to the way women were depicted in textbooks, and especially in the basal readers used in nearly every elementary classroom. It was pointed out that, although women and girls formed slightly more than half the population of the United States, they were a distinct minority in textbooks. Also, in a period in which women were increasingly seeking and finding careers, often in occupations formerly the exclusive property of men, women in textbooks were depicted predominantly as housewives or in the few traditional female occupations—nurse, teacher, secretary—and women and girls were most frequently shown in passive, subservient roles. Typically, beginning basal readers showed boys climbing, playing baseball, running and helping their fathers in active occupations, while girls looked on, encouraged the boys, helped make cookies, and gave tea parties for their pets.

Today, many textbooks show a new awareness of women's widening roles and present more realistic pictures of girls as positive, active participants and protagonists in a wide range of activities. These texts better reflect the society in which their readers are growing up and better indicate the many options, social and occupational, open to both girls and boys.

How well have texts in the past reflected their societies? How accurately did they depict life during the dynamic years of growth on the North American continent? What did they teach girls and boys about the world around them? What philosophies and purposes guided their writing? A look at some of the books of the past 200 years may help to provide answers.

While all textbooks provide clues, reading texts are especially sensitive to the spirit of a given period because reading, unlike other school subjects, has no content of its own. Reading skills cannot be taught without the use of words and sentences. The choice of these words and sentences can be expected to reveal much about the purposes, interests, and controlling ideas of text writers. For example, the first American reading text, *The New England Primer*, first published in the late 17th century, includes *for-ni-ca-ti-on*—a wildly improbable choice until one realizes that the main purpose of teaching reading at that time was to prepare children to read the Bible.

In examining texts of the past, it is convenient to use four of the periods of reading instruction delineated by Nila Banton Smith in her seminal history, *American Reading Instruction*. These are the periods of Religious Emphasis (c. 1680-c. 1776), the period of National-Moralistic Emphasis (c. 1776-c. 1840), the period of Emphasis on Education for Intelligent Citizenship (c. 1840-c. 1880), and the period of Reading as a Cultural Asset (c. 1880-c. 1910). Smith does not stop with 1910 but her last three periods, from 1910 until 1965, are essentially periods of different kinds of methodology and research emphases rather than of content. Let us consider some of the materials from these periods as reflectors of their societies. Especially, let us look at their treatment of men and women and boys and girls.

The Period of Religious Emphasis

The title of the period tells it all. Reading was taught to enable people to read the Bible, "It being one chief point of that old deluder, Satan, to keep men (*sic*) from a knowledge of the scriptures," as expressed by a Massachusetts law of 1647. The most widely used text throughout the period was *The New England Primer,* issued in many editions over a period of more than 100 years. Although best known for its picture alphabet ("In Adam's fall/We sinned all"), it also included a variety of other features, nearly all of them religious. My own copy, a facsimile printed in 1887 of a Boston edition of 1777, starts with two prayers, continues with the alphabet (in both roman and italic type) and a page of syllables (ab, eb, ib, ob, ub; ba, be, bi, bo, bu; etc.); lists words of one, two, three, four, five, and six syllables; and immediately goes on to "A Lesson for Children" which starts out with admonitions to "Pray to God," "Love God," "Fear God," "Serve God," and "Take Not God's Name in Vain." The rest of the book is entirely religious with two exceptions, a list of men's and women's names ("to teach Children to spell their own") and a four line verse ("Learn these four lines by heart"): "Have communion with few, / Be intimate with one, / Deal justly with all, / Speak evil of none." There are hymns, prayers, religious verses, another religious alphabet, two different catechisms, and a catechism like Bible quiz.

The book is strongly male centered. The picture alphabet includes the names of eighteen men—from Adam to Zaccheus—and three women—Esther, Ruth, and Vashti. The list of men's names includes 109; that of women's names, 62. It is Adam's fall that has condemned humankind; Eve isn't even mentioned.

How well does all this reflect the society that produced it? The answer is not simple. Certainly New England was a religious society; both the Pilgrims and the Puritans came to North America for reasons primarily religious. Religion was a strong interest. But it was not the only interest of these energetic men and women. Many Puritans were ambitious and successful business people. None of this aptitude for worldly success and none of the Puritans' love of beautiful silver, furniture, and architecture (Morison, p. 62) comes through in *The New England Primer*. Instead, Puritan children learned that "While youth do chear/Death may be near." The reflection is there, but it is imperfect. Like the "night" position on a day-night rear view mirror, *The New England Primer* reflects selectively, omitting much but highlighting that which was important to the dominant group in the society at the time. Instead of mirroring daily life, it suggests an ideal life—what these dominant people wished their lives were like and hoped their children's would be. The same can probably be said of later materials, even those of today. They reflect not what we are (or were) but some of our ideals, aspirations, and weaknesses. They show what we think we would like to be or to have been.

The Period of National Moralistic Emphasis (c. 1776 - c. 1840)

After the Revolutionary War, American schoolbooks began to broaden their subject matter and decrease the emphasis on religion. Politics came to replace religion at the center of society. The purposes of reading instruction changed to match the new emphasis. The aim of reading instruction now was to "purify the American language; to develop loyalty to the new nation. . .; and to inculcate the high ideas of virtue and moral behavior which were considered so necessary a part of the general program of building good citizenship" (Smith, 1963, p. 37). In keeping with this aim, reading texts of the period emphasized works by American writers and, especially in the case of the schoolbooks by Noah Webster, put great stress on correct usage and pronunciation. They also presented patriotic and historical selections and plenty of speeches, for the ability to speak in public was considered a desirable and necessary accomplishment for citizens of a republic.

And they were moralistic. Webster's *Grammatical Institute* (1783-1785) contained such reading lessons as:

> A good child will not lie, swear, nor steal. He [sic] will be good at home, and ask to read his book; when he gets up he will wash his hands and face clean; he will comb his hair and make haste to school; he will not play by the way as bad boys do.
> As for those boys and girls that mind not their books and love not the church and school, but play with such as tell lies, curse, swear, and steal, they will come to some bad end and must be whipt till they mend their ways.

There was a "moral Catechism" that included such questions as "Is pride commendable?" and its answer: "By no means. A modest, self-approving opinion of our own good deeds is very right. . . .But we should not suffer our hearts to be blown up with pride; for pride brings upon us the ill-will of mankind and displeasure of our Maker" (Johnson, pp. 177, 180).

Girls fared somewhat better in the books of this period, at least in terms of being represented. But the sexes were depicted stereotypically. Webster's *Grammatical Institute* includes the following:

> The little boy chuses some plaything that will make a noise, a hammer, a stick, or a whip. The little girl loves her doll and learns to dress it (Johnson, p. 177).

Girls were welcomed at the schools, but their education was not taken seriously by many. For example, in "A Dialogue between Miss Charlotte and Miss Sophia" in Caleb Bingham's *The Child's Companion* (which had gone through 20 editions by 1832), Charlotte, who has taken her "work" to school but has left her spelling book home, wonders at Sophia's devotion to spelling: "Mamma says that if they do but know what we *mean*, that is enough." Later, however, she admits that her bad spelling got her into difficulties when, instead of writing "For Sally Chapman" in a book she was sending her cousin, she wrote, "For Sale Cheap Mon" which was translated by the recipient as, "For sale cheap for money." She agrees that she will now "ask Mamma to let me carry my spelling book to school each day" (Johnson, pp. 187-188).

Despite such selections as this, most of the reading material was for and about boys. It was for them that school was considered important. "The glimpse we get of Charlotte's mother (in the above dialogue mirrors the general opinion of the times that it was hardly worthwhile to teach girls much except sewing and housework, and if they took their stitching to school, it did not matter much if they left their spellers at home" (Johnson, p. 189). Another example of contemporary attitudes toward the sexes is seen in a lesson apparently on homonyms in an 1836 speller published in Portland, Maine: "Boys *need* dinner; girls *knead* dough" (quoted in Johnson, p. 228).

These books, like those of the previous period, reflect part of their society, but only part of it. The arrival of some 670,000 immigrants, the new settlements in the West (in which women worked side by side with men and often cleared land, grew crops, and reared children alone when their husbands died or were away on extended trips), and the steady erosion of relations between the North and the South are not even hinted at. Nor is the growing movement for better education for women, represented by the pioneer work of Emma Willard and Mary Lyon, nor the rapid development of the factory system and the increasing urbanization of the country. Instead, we find in Webster's *The Little Reader's Assistant,* "What is the *best* business a man can do? Tilling the ground, or farming. Why is farming the best business? Because it is the most necessary, the most innocent, and the most agreeable employment of men" (quoted in Johnson, p. 276).

The Period of Emphasis on Education for Intelligent Citizenship (c. 1840-1880)

In this period, reading materials began to shift toward more informational selections in keeping with a realization on the part of educators "that the success of the new democracy depended not so largely upon arousing patriotic sentiment as upon developing the intelligence of the people, whose ballots were to choose its leaders and determine its policies" (Smith, 1963, p. 75). Upper grade readers had selections dealing with science, history, and other subjects; beginning readers contained many stories about nature. Animals are often anthropomorphized, and a strain of sentimentality is apparent in many of the selections, but for the first time there appears to be a genuine attempt to provide materials that will interest children.

A parallel goal to providing information was developing oral reading and elocutionary skills. (Until late in this period, virtually all reading instruction was in terms of oral reading; reading aloud was a favorite family entertainment, and good oral readers were prized.) Literature was provided in upper grade readers primarily to be read aloud or memorized and recited. In many of its selections, *Osgood's American Fourth Reader* (1872) includes accent marks to indicate rising and falling inflection.

This text is an interesting example of the reading books of the period. It contains such "classics" as "The Boy Stood on the Burning Deck" and Lewis Carroll's "The Mock Turtle's Story" ("...reeling and writhing...fainting in coils"), a number of pious selections on the evils of drink, and an inspirational essay called

"Dig for Knowledge as Men Dig for Gold" which starts with the admonition:

> Away, young man, with all dreams of superiority unless you are determined to dig after knowledge as men search for concealed gold!

and continues,

> Up, then, young man, and gird yourself for the work of self-cultivation. . . . The great thoughts of great men are now to be procured at prices almost nominal. You can, therefore, easily collect a library of choice standard works. But above all, learn to reflect even more than you read. . . . Let thought and reading go hand in hand, and the intellect will rapidly increase in strength and gifts. Its possessor will rise in character, in power, and in positive influence (Osgood, pp. 242-243).

Most of the selections in this book are male-centered. But, curiously, the most interesting and ingenious action story in the book has a woman as its central character. The story is of a builder who gets marooned on top of a tall chimney, "one of those lofty chimneys which, in our manufacturing towns, almost supply the place of other architectural beauty." Through an oversight, the rope, down which the builder was to climb after the scaffolding had been removed, had never been taken up. How was he to descend? Enter his wife. "Take off thy stocking, lad, and unravel it," she shouted up to him. "Let down the thread with a bit of mortar." This being done, mason's twine is attached to the thread and pulled up, then rope to the mason's twine, and down comes the builder, no worse for wear, thanks to his wife's resourcefulness (Osgood, pp. 246-251).

This story is not only the only one to show a woman in an active, positive situation, it is also the only one to even hint at the industrialization that was going on all over America. There is no hint in this book of the Civil War, less than ten years in the past, or the telegraph, or the work of Susan B. Anthony and Elizabeth Cady Stanton, or any of the myriad events that had happened or were happening in those postwar years.

Another reader of the period, *Monroe's Fifth Reader* (1871) has a much more literary emphasis, with works by a wide variety of authors including Hawthorne, Whittier, Henry Ward Beecher, Louisa May Alcott, Longfellow, Tennyson, and Byron.

Like the Osgood book, it is essentially male-oriented; the Alcott excerpt, featuring Beth, Meg, Jo, and Amy from *Little Women*, is a refreshing exception. Typically, however, girls and women are bystanders. A delightful story by Jacob Abbott (a children's author and innovative educator of the period) is told from the viewpoint of two girls, but they are strictly observers of a little drama: Two bad boys remain unaffected by a severe scolding but are defused by the wiles of a young man who is obviously a born teacher and a natural psychologist (Monroe, pp. 40-46).

Here again, the society that is pictured is pastoral and male centered. What was actually going on in America is not represented at all.

The Period of Reading as a Cultural Asset (c. 1880 - c. 1910)

The emphasis in this period is on literature. The Monroe book cited above belongs as much to this as to the previous period in which it was actually published. It had become important for Americans to appear cultured. They were tired of being portrayed by European visitors as unlettered bumpkins and barbarians. They were to learn to read so they could absorb and appreciate the great writers, both English and American, and the materials they used were directed to this purpose. Of these, the McGuffey series is the archetype.

This series bridges the gap between the period of Emphasis on Education for Intelligent Citizenship and that of Reading as a Cultural Asset, for it was first published in the late 1830s; its last revision was in the 1920s. Only *The New England Primer* endured as long. Moralistic, patriotic, and literary, it offered something to everyone and helped form the minds and literary tastes of millions of Americans. McGuffey, a brilliant educator, was among the first to control vocabulary and provide ample repetition of new words. He was also a perceptive anthologist, and the literary quality in his texts outshone that of his competitors. Perhaps most of all, McGuffey and his publishers knew what the market wanted, which was a smattering of knowledge of nearly every important English and American writer, together with a seasoning of patriotic material (speeches by Patrick Henry and Daniel Webster) and religious matter (excerpts from the Bible). The list of authors includes 111 names, from Addison to Wordsworth. Among the 111 are 8 women.

Obviously, the McGuffey books are male centered. In this same Sixth Reader, out of 138 selections, 5 concern women or girls. In one, the male author suggests that girls or women never appear half so lovely as they do when "gayly convened at the work-covered table, / Each cheerfully active, playing her part, / Beguiling the task with a song or a fable, / And plying the needle with exquisite art." Another, also by a male, makes fun of the housewife's annual spring cleaning and the havoc it creates for the husband who is forced to "abdicate for a time, and run from an evil which he can neither prevent nor mollify" (McGuffey, pp. 67, 73).

The periods from 1840 to 1880 and from 1880 to 1910 were periods of unparallelled dynamism in the history of the United States. Manifest Destiny was in the air; the fruits of the Industrial Revolution were being harvested; the conflict between the North and the South came to a head and was finally, it seemed, resolved; the "Indian Question" was well on its way to its final bloody answer. The United States was becoming a major world power. America was on the move!

How much of this hustle and bustle, of this rapidly changing panorama, is reflected in the readers of the period? At first glance, the answer would seem to be, "almost none." There is no hint of the teeming activity and the squalor of the mushrooming cities; of the children forced to work in dangerous, noisy factories; of the vast fortunes made and lost; or of the backbreaking labor of the Oriental immigrants who built the transcontinental railroads. We do not hear about the growth of the labor movement or the clamor for women's suffrage. Nor do we hear about the problems of reconstruction or, before the Civil War, those of slavery. Instead, we see a rural countryside populated for the most part by middle class white males, an America summed up by George Inness' Metropolitan Museum painting, "Peace and Plenty."

But these readers, even though they do not mirror events and movements, do reflect the values and attitudes of the dominant group. They reflect an unbounded optimism; a firm belief in the perfectability of humankind; and, above all, a faith in the American dream. To the reading educators of these periods, and to most of the public they addressed, America really did promise Peace and Plenty. Once more, the mirror was selective, reflecting what was important to the viewer and filtering out the rest.

Yesterday and Today

What about contemporary reading materials? Do they come any closer to reflecting our society than those of 100 years ago reflected theirs? Again, there is no simple answer. In certain ways, today's readers do a far better job of reflecting their world than did any published earlier. In other ways, however, they present an image just as incomplete and distorted as that shown in *The New England Primer*.

To see how far we have come, we need look only at the readers of the 1950s and 1960s. *The New Fun with Dick and Jane* (Scott, Foresman, 1951), except for its illustrations, might have been produced in 1870 as far as the depicted society and incidents are concerned. The exceptions are the presence of the family car in two of the stories and of a bus in one story. Otherwise, nothing has changed. The characters are all white, upper middle class, and live in a small town or suburb. Dick flies a kite, rescues Baby Sally from a rainstorm, and plays with boats. Jane plays with dolls: her ambition is to have a doll that talks.

By the late 1960s, American mutiethnicism had been accepted by textbook purchasers and publishers. Dick and Jane and Sally had been joined by Mike and Pam and Penny, black children. The civil rights movement and the resulting civil rights acts of 1957 and 1964, together with the 1957 Supreme Court decision banning "separate but equal" schools, were responsible for this change. Other series also included Blacks, Orientals, Hispanics, and other minority groups, sometimes as central figures in stories. Despite this most of the stories in all series continued to portray an essentially white, middle class society.

Sex role stereotyping persisted throughout this period. Not until the mid-to-late 1970s did this begin to change. The change was rapid, however. Just as the civil rights movement of the 1950s and 1960s was fundamentally responsible for the appearance of blacks and other minorities in textbooks, so the women's movement of the 1960s and 1970s was responsible for the rush toward elimination of sexual stereotypes and sexist language in readers.

It was a rush because well-prepared leaders of women's groups protested reading adoptions in key areas, a publicity campaign sparked by these groups had alerted the public to the sexual stereotypes in existing reading series, and many reading editors in publishing houses were in sympathy with the women's movement and ready to act.

Since 1975, authors and publishers of reading series have attempted, with greater or lesser success, to eliminate sex stereotyping in both text and illustrations. For example, in the readers of the 1950s and 1960s, adult females are usually homemakers, teachers, or nurses. In current readers, they are astronomers, veterinarians, architects, writers, computer pro-gramers, doctors—and homemakers, teachers, and nurses. In the older readers, girls and women were almost invariably shown wearing skirts or dresses. Little girls, in particular, always looked as if they were dressed for a party. In current editions, jeans and slacks are frequently seen while aprons, once the hallmark of every mother, have nearly faded into oblivion.

Girls and women occupy central roles in many stories in today's readers. Macmillan's *Series r*, which first appeared in 1975, features many female centered stories, especially in comparison with Macmillan's previous series in which one third grade text had twelve male centered stories compared to four female centered stories. Allyn and Bacon's *Sheldon Reading Series* (1973) had a male-female ratio of about two to one; the same publisher's *Pathfinder* series (1978) has a one-to-one ratio both in stories and in illustration "head count." Similar comparisons can be made between the pre-1975 and post-1975 readers of almost all publishers.

The readers reflect our world in other ways, also. Blacks, Hispanics, Asian Americans, and American Indians are well represented in natural, integrated situations; the cultural heritage of these and other minority groups is recognized to a lesser degree. Almost all readers show the technical side of life—airplanes, automobiles, trucks, television, and space and undersea exploration. There are articles on consumer education and propaganda analysis and a strong emphasis on contemporary and recent sports heroes.

Another deviation from the readers of just a few years earlier is an emphasis on ecology. Most current readers have stories that directly or indirectly concern the environment and our relationship to it. Nor are such stories confined to the upper grades; one series has a biography of Rachel Carson in a second grade book.

Many readers attempt to deal with the idea of death. Miska Miles' "Annie and the Old One" appears in several series, and other stories touch on death. Perhaps related to this are occasional stories about the very old, a subject conspicuously lacking in earlier readers.

What is missing, then? Poverty. There are no families on welfare in basal readers, and none living in slum housing projects. Some other omissions are the following.

Racial conflict. Although many series contain stories of discrimination in the past (up to and including the Montgomery, Alabama, bus boycott), there is little about the continuing conflicts between blacks and whites. (Articles on the Watts Towers in Los Angeles gloss over the fact that Watts was the scene of racially motivated riots.)

Politics. There is no hint of Watergate; of the routinely accepted political corruption in most large cities; or of the kinds of trade-offs that, while accepted as legal tender on Capitol Hill, may drastically affect the lives of millions of Americans. Such political figures as are shown—mayors, often—are represented either as eagerly responsive or as humorously muddleheaded.

Sex. Thousands of twelve and thirteen year olds are sexually active. Millions more are concerned about how to handle their sexual feelings. One need only read newspaper advice columns or examine statistics on teenage pregnancy to know that this is an area of extreme importance to many fifth and sixth grade students. Yet basal readers completely ignore sex.

Religion. Occasional stories mention Christmas or Passover, but these are rare, and they are usually concerned with the secular aspects of these occasions rather than with the religious. No one in primary readers goes to church or temple.

Preaching or moralizing. Virtue does triumph, to be sure (agencies adopting books look for moral and spiritual values in readers), but the moral lessons are taught subtly and implicitly rather than by the kind of explicit exhortation found in the 1870 readers.

Today's Reading Materials and
Today's Society: In Summary

It seems obvious that while present day readers portray their society more realistically and present more aspects of it than did those of the past, they omit a number of elements. Two of the three social revolutions of our time, the civil rights movement and the women's movement, receive some kind of recognition; the third, the sexual revolution, does not. An occasional story may mention divorce or present a one parent family but no series deals with sex in any way. Even the most innocuous heterosexual romance fails to find its way into readers.

This selective reflection appears once more to result from a coming together of the values and attitudes of the dominant groups in the period and the authors' purposes in teaching reading. In assessing these, we lack the advantage of historical perspective; our tentative estimates may seem naive or misguided fifty years from now. Some kind of estimate seems in order, however.

As far as the spirit that is reflected is concerned, this appears to be one of emphasis on the individual American. While one side of this has produced the phenomenon referred to as the "me generation," another has focused on individual dignity and worth. The age of the homogenized, mass-produced American—symbolized by blond Dick and Jane, living in never-never land—is over. In its stead is an age in which individual human beings are considered as individuals. Ethnic background is seen paradoxically as 1) of no importance and 2) something to be proud of.

Whether one is male or female is considered irrelevant as far as aspirations are concerned. This is the spirit shown in readers, and perhaps it is closer to what we believe than might seem to be the case at first glance.

An examination of today's readers suggests that the author's principal purpose for teaching reading is to help young people's personal development, although this is not explicitly stated in the materials. As a part of this purpose, programs aim to build a love of reading. They also present role models for children both through biographical material about persons of diverse backgrounds and through fiction featuring young people from a variety of ethnic groups and socioeconomic levels (the exception is true poverty). Through story interest and questions and activities in pupils' books and teachers' guides, children are encouraged to identify with story characters and their problems and ways of solving them.

Reading is also seen as a way to broaden children's conceptual backgrounds, especially at the primary level, by introducing them to a variety of things, people, and places, of which they might otherwise be unaware.

Perhaps this vision of reading as personality development has been an underlying motive for the teaching of reading ever since reading began to be taught. But in association with the current emphasis on the individual, it is being expressed in different ways. There is a greater emphasis on the enjoyment of reading as an end in itself; there is more of an attempt to portray girls and boys and men and women in some of the typical situations in which modern life often places them; and there is greater emphasis on helping children understand and empathize with the feelings of others—old or young, male or female, white or black or from another ethnic group.

Reading materials today are still selective reflectors. They do not mirror their world; there is no one-to-one correspondence. But they do reflect some important aspects of it, and the view they present is broader and more comprehensive than the view of society presented by earlier readers. It is less sexist and more humane. If children accept this view, if they come to accept all human beings as equal in potential, perhaps they can grow up to help remake society to more closely conform to this view. If reading can truly help to bring about a new attitude toward the world and the people in it, then we can say, with the author of *The New England Primer*, "My Book and Heart/Shall Never Part."

References

Gray, William S., et al. *New fun with Dick and Jane*. Chicago: Scott, Foresman, 1951.

Harris, Albert J., and Mae Knight Clark. *More than words*. New York: Macmillan, 1974.

Johnson, Clifton. *Old time schools and schoolbooks*. New York: Dover, 1963.

McGuffey's sixth eclectic reader, Revised Edition. New York: American Book, 1921.

Monroe, Lewis B. *The fifth reader*. Philadelphia: Cowperthwait, 1871.

Morison, Samuel Eliot. *The Oxford history of the American people*. New York: Oxford University Press, 1965.

Osgood, Lucius. *Osgood's American fourth reader for schools and families*. New York: Taintor Brothers, 1872.

Robinson, Helen M., et al. *Teacher's edition for preprimers*. Chicago: Scott, Foresman, 1965.

Ruddell, Robert B., et al. *Pathfinder: Allyn and Bacon reading program*. Boston: Allyn and Bacon, 1978.

Sheldon, William D., et al. *Sheldon reading series, pacing edition*. Boston: Allyn and Bacon, 1973.

Smith, Carl B., et al. *Series r: The new Macmillan reading program*. New York: Macmillan, 1975.

Smith, Nila Banton. *American reading instruction*. Newark, Delaware: International Reading Association, 1963.

A Feminist Look at Literature
for Children: Ten Years Later

Ramona S. Frasher

The subject of sexism and sex role stereotyping in children's reading material has been the subject of much discussion during the past decade. In the early seventies many writers criticized the content of children's literature for its inequitable, inaccurate, and biased portrayal of the sexes, particularly females (Feminists on Children's Literature, 1971; Key, 1971; Stewig and Higgs, 1973; Weitzman, et al., 1972). These articles, along with many students of children's textbooks, pinpointed the patterns that led to those accusations: 1) unequal quantitative representation, with male characters outnumbering females; 2) extreme traditional stereotyping of behavior and personality, with females depicted as subordinate, passive observers frequently preoccupied with domestic and romantic concerns and males portrayed as active, competent leaders engaged in interesting and challenging tasks; 3) generally negative attitudes toward females, including denigrating statements about girls, women, and feminine behavior; and 4) males represented in a variety of occupational roles and females severely restricted to a small number of occupations (Frasher and Walker, 1972; Oliver, 1974; Taylor, 1973; Weitzman and Rizzo, 1975; Women on Words and Images, 1972; Zimet, 1973).

Generally these authors agreed that materials reflecting such patterns had serious potential for harmful effects on children's—especially girls'—attitudes, self-concepts, and aspirations. Furthermore, widespread credibility for these claims and acceptance of the need for change developed rapidly. Major publishers of books for children—including Ginn (1975), Holt, Rinehart & Winston (1975), Houghton Mifflin (1975), Lippincott (DeBoard et al., 1975), McGraw-Hill (1974), Macmillan (1975), and Scott, Foresman (Sexism in Textbooks Committee, 1972)— issued guidelines for eliminating sex bias. Professional organizations issued resolutions or statements supporting sex equity in materials for children, published guidelines for publications, and developed strategies for combating stereotypes and sexism in educational materials (Association for Supervision and Curriculum Development, 1975; International Reading Association, 1977; National Council of Teachers of English, 1976; National Educational Association, 1973). Contemporary textbooks for preservice and inservice teacher education programs address the need for awareness of sex bias in evaluating, selecting, and using materials for children. Two recently published texts on children's literature devote entire sections to the treatment of females in books (Rudman, 1976; Sadker and Sadker, 1977); others include discussions of the topics of sexism and stereotyping (Glazer and Williams, 1979; Huck, 1979; Tiedt, 1979).

Has a decade of awareness and intent produced changes in the treatment of the sexes in children's literature? If so, how do recent books portray females and males with respect to the areas of criticism described above? A survey of recently published books, popular selection aids, and replications of earlier studies points out some of the trends that have emerged.

Award Books

An early critique pointed out that in Newbery Award winning books, male main characters outnumbered female main characters by about three to one and that sexism and stereotyping were blatant in many (Feminists on Children's Literature, 1971). An analysis of Caldecott Award winning picture books resulted in similar conclusions; more males than females were featured and roles were highly stereotyped (Weitzman et al., 1972). In the following section, sex roles and representation in the award winning books for the past decade are discussed.

The Feminists on Children's Literature defined nonsexist children's literature in the following statement: "In our view, a nonsexist portrayal would offer the girl reader a positive image of women's physical, emotional, and intellectual potential—one that would encourage her to reach her own full personhood, free of traditionally imposed limitations" (1971, p. 19). This definition, as valid today as when it first appeared, was used as a standard for the evaluation of the female main characters featured in the Newbery books.

Table 1
NEWBERY AWARD WINNERS, 1971-1980

Year	Title	Sex of M.C.
1971	Summer of the Swans	Female
1972	Mrs. Frisby and the Rats of NIMH	Female
1973	Julie of the Wolves	Female
1974	The Slave Dancer	Male
1975	M.C. Higgins the Great	Male
1976	The Grey King	Male
1977	Roll of Thunder, Hear My Cry	Female
1978	Bridge to Terabithia	Male
1979	The Westing Game	---
1980	A Gathering of Days	Female

Table 1 lists the Newbery Award winners with the sex of the main characters indicated for all titles except the 1979 award book, which will be discussed at a later point in this section. In the remaining nine books, the ratio for sex of main character favors females, five to four. This clearly reflects a quantitative improvement over representation of the sexes in previous Newbery books.

In two instances, 1972 and 1977, I have indicated that the main characters are female even though their roles do not dominate. They are categorized thusly because they serve a major function in moving or narrating the events in their respective stories. Mrs. Frisby (1972) fulfills the largely stereotyped role of a concerned mother (mouse). During most of the story she is overshadowed by her male rodent counterparts, who solve her problem for her. Although she is responsible for saving the lives of some of her friends by warning them of impending disaster, she does not represent the positive image described in the definition of nonsexist portrayal.

Cassie's role (1977) is primarily that of a narrator of the events that happen around her and her family in the South during 1930s. A bright, outspoken and active girl, she struggles to understand and cope with the injustices that plague her, her family, her friends, and all other black people in a segregated and discriminatory society. Cassie is a positive model for she shows strength, courage, and a depth of understanding not typical of the stereotyped storybook girl. Her mother, a prominent character, presents a strong and admirable adult model for her daughter and for the readers of *Roll of Thunder, Hear My Cry*.

Sara Godfrey (1971) is beset by typical adolescent self-consciousness; she is a very realistic protagonist. She also displays great strength and determination in searching for and finding her lost younger brother. However, one of her major conflicts is resolved through the beginning of a potentially romantic relationship with a boy who comes to her aid (a happy, if somewhat contrived, resolution far too familiar in books about adolescents). Sara's positive characteristics represent an improvement over the stereotyped adolescent girl characters that formerly dominated books for this age level. However, the book leaves the impression that Sara's social and emotional growth has depended on Joe's interest and intervention to a greater extent than on her own attemts to work out her problems.

Julie (1973) is clearly the female most liberated from the traditional trappings of literary femininity. She is a strong, brave, and resourceful girl who resists and escapes a traditional sex role prescribed by her Eskimo culture—early marriage—and survives in the harsh Alaskan wilderness. Although she has to depend on a pack of wolves for food and companionship, Julie is not a passive recipient of their gifts. She works hard to communicate with them, to make them accept her. There is no question that Julie's survival and her future are in her own hands.

The protagonist of *A Gathering of Days* (1980) is traditional within the context of the early 19th century setting of the story. A competent and industrious girl, Catherine's integrity is revealed when she decides to help a fleeing slave, but only after prodding by a young male friend. Her strongest hint of feminist leaning is a wistful wondering whether her father would have given her his Barlow knife if he had not acquired a stepson through marriage.

In *The Westing Game* (1979), each character introduced plays a significant role in the development of the plot; thus, there is no one main character. Each person also portrays a "special" segment of American society; a variety of ages, occupations, socioeconomic levels, the handicapped, and three racial groups are represented. In addition to diverse and interesting roles for males, the array includes a host of prominent females, including several who evolve from traditional stereotypes to successful individuals. A social climbing housewife becomes a restaurateur, a timid bride-to-be postpones her marriage in favor of going to college and medical school, and a submissive Chinese wife/cook becomes a successful business executive. This book also has a female judge who ends up on the Supreme Court. And the mystery of the Westing Game is solved by a precocious little girl whose favorite pastime is playing the stock market. Although not a serious portrayal of people and events, this story is unique in its representation of females in significant, interesting, and unusual roles.

Because of the preponderance of folk literature and animal characters in the Caldecott Award winning books, it is more difficult to analyze sex roles. Females figure prominently as the focus of activity in three of the books receiving the award during the past decade (1973, 1974, 1979); males, including animals, are featured in five (1971, 1972, 1975, 1978, 1980); and no main character is featured in either the 1976 or 1977 winners. Table 2 lists the Caldecott winners for the years 1971 through 1980.

No nonsexist stories are represented in this list. *Duffy and the Devil* (1974) comes closer than any of the others, for Duffy enlists the aid of her witch-housekeeper in outwitting the devil

Table 2
CALDECOTT AWARD WINNERS, 1971-1980

Year	Title	Sex of M.C.
1971	A Story, A Story	Male
1972	One Fine Day	Male
1973	The Funny Little Woman	Female
1974	Duffy and the Devil	Female
1975	Arrow to the Sun	Male
1976	Why Mosquitoes Buzz in People's Ears	---
1977	Ashanti to Zulu	---
1978	Noah's Ark	Male
1979	The Girl Who Loved Wild Horses	Female
1980	Ox-Cart Man	Male

and is nontraditional in terms of her decision not to be bogged down with domestic tasks; but this book is no model of positive images. The witch stereotype and the gullibility and dependence of the female main character make this variant of Rumpelstiltskin nothing more than a funny version of a familiar theme. *The Funny Little Woman* (1973) is the essence of silliness; the funny little woman was saved from a lifetime of cooking for ogres but not from a lifetime of cooking. *The Girl Who Loved Wild Horses* (1979) escapes to a life she loves, but she does not control her own fate. A wild stallion becomes her master, defending her like one of his herd.

In *Arrow to the Sun* (1975), a woman is used as the ultimate stereotype—to give birth to the Boy Arrow who brings the Sun spirit to his people. Her role is negligible, however, as are the roles of females who appear in the backgrounds of some of the other books. *Ashanti to Zulu*, the alphabet book that won the 1977 award, does have a balanced representation of the sexes in its illustrations, but it depicts cultures in which sex roles are strongly dichotomized.

Like its Newbery counterpart, the most recent Caldecott Award winner presents a very traditional picture of sex roles in early nineteenth century New England. But just as a touch of feminism emerges in Catherine's longing for her father's knife, a touch of the nontraditional emerges when the ox-cart man kisses his ox goodbye.

In summary, it may be concluded that both quantitative and qualitative improvement in the treatment of females is reflected in one category of award books—those designed for the older child. Recent Newbery Award winners present positive and varied images of women in enough instances to constitute a trend. The same cannot be said about the Caldecott books, which as a group continue to be replete with stereotypes.

Although the award winning books represent the best in literature for children and receive a great deal of publicity, credibility, and attention as a result of the honor bestowed on them, they do not represent the scope of books published for children during the years the medals were awarded. Other approaches to evaluating sex roles in literature are necessary in order to assess progress in the area.

Comparative Investigations

Stewig and his coauthors, who conducted two studies of sex roles in picture books, reported little change (Stewig and Higgs, 1973; Stewig and Knipfel, 1975). In the books examined in the earlier study, 84 percent of the women were portrayed in homemaking roles; in the later study, 68 percent of the books showed women in homemaking roles. Consistent with the earlier report, men in books analyzed in the 1975 study were depicted as more active than women and appeared in a greater variety of occupational roles. These results are also consistent with the results of the Caldecott analysis; together they present a rather dismal outlook with respect to progress in improving the status of females in books for young children.

However, a great many picture books have been published since the later Stewig study was conducted, and it is possible that a current analysis of this category would reflect change. This suggestion is prompted particularly by the appearance of lengthy bibliographies of nonsexist picture books, including those by Adell and Klein (1976) and Bissett (1979) as well as the one that appears in this volume.

Patterns of sex bias were also found in an investigation that involved the analysis of reading and social studies series as well as literature textbooks for grades one through twelve. Britton and Lumpkin (1977) examined 16,176 selections, comparing those published during "preguideline" years (1958-1970) with those published during "postguideline" years (1974-1976). Sixty percent of the preguideline stories had male main characters; 61 percent of the postguideline stories featured males. Stories with female main characters only increased from 14 percent to 16 percent. These authors also reported that career roles were as sex stereotyped in the recently published texts as in those published before guidelines on sex bias were issued.

However, a recent study following the Britton and Lumpkin procedures in an analysis of 1976, 1977, and 1978 reading textbooks reflects considerably more change (Longnion and Garcia, n.d.). Stories classified as "Female Dominant" increased to 18 percent and stories classified as "Male Dominant" decreased to 33 percent. Because this report did not discuss the types of roles of males or females it is not possible to ascertain whether careers, personality types, and behaviors were represented across both sexes. It does, however, reflect significant improvement in quantitative representation of the sexes.

Book reviews and selection aids reflect current publishing trends. Although they can provide a limited amount of information, in most cases it is possible to ascertain at least the sex of main characters. In many instances it is also possible to identify distinctive characteristics of the protagonists. I conducted a simple survey of sex of main characters in fiction and individual biographies listed in the 1969 and 1979 supplements to the *Children's Catalog* (1969, 1979), a selection aid in widespread use by children's librarians. The entries in an annual supplement consist of recent titles reviewed and recommended by professional librarians and include brief descriptive and critical comments. Table 3 shows that the percentage of female main characters in fiction increased during that period. However, during the same period the percentage of biographies of women decreased.

Table 3

REPRESENTATION OF MALES AND FEMALES
IN *Children's Catalog* SUPPLEMENTS

Year	Male	Female
	Fiction	
1969	53 (63%)	31 (37%)
1979	50 (56%)	39 (44%)
	Biography	
1969	14 (82%)	3 (18%)
1979	7 (100%)	0 (0%)

Noyce (1976) conducted a more extensive study of 657 reviews of children's fiction that appeared in the *Bulletin of the Center for Children's Books* during 1975 and 1976. She found an even smaller disparity between numbers of males and females represented as main characters—331 female (49.2 percent) and 342 male (50.8 percent) protagonists. Noyce also assigned one characteristic describing the main character in each story. Males were assigned positive characteristics in 314 stories; females, in 290. Moreover, males and females were almost equally represented in all of the positive categories except "courageous" (43 males to 28 females). Few negative traits were assigned (68), but females were assigned more than males (60 percent to 40 percent).

In general, these surveys reflect progress toward achieving greater equity in the number of main character roles represented by females and males. The Noyce analysis also reflects a trend toward more positive and varied personality characteristics for females in fiction, a trend that also appeared in the analysis of Newbery books.

Occupations and Careers

Occupational roles of adults in fiction and models representing jobs and professions in career educational materials have been criticized harshly for their extreme sex role stereotyping. Women rarely appeared other than as mother-homemaker, teacher, nurse, secretary, or clerk, a factor that critics suggested implied to young readers that these occupations were the only ones appropriate for women or that women were capable of filling.

According to studies by Stewig and Knipfel (1975) and Britton and Lumpkin (1977), this pattern had not changed signficantly in picture books and textbooks by the mid-seventies. At this point no analysis of occupational roles in recent fiction for older children has been published. However, the category of career books for children and young people has experienced a noticeable change; namely, the publication of books that specifically feature females in nontraditional and varied occupations. Merriam's *Mommies at Work* (1961) predated the move to feature women in a broader scope of roles and for nearly a decade was the only such book for young children. It was followed by a string of books with a similar purpose. Some, such as Rothman's *I Can Be Anything You Can Be* (1973) and Laskey's *Mothers Can Do Anything* (1972), are somewhat didactic; others, such as Rockwell's *My Doctor* (1973) integrate women in nontraditional roles in a less contrived fashion. Now entire series and numerous single titles have appeared on careers for females. The series, *Choosing Career and Lifestyles* (published by J. Watts) and *What Can She Be?* (published by Lothrop, Lee, and Shepherd) and the books *I Can Be Anything* (Mitchell, 1978) and *Women at Their Work* (English, 1977) are representative examples.

A similar phenomenon has appeared with respect to biographies of women for older children. Despite the fact that no entries for individual biographies of women appeared in the 1979 supplement to the *Children's Catalog*, the section on collective biographies for that year included two entries and the *Junior High School Library* 1979 supplement listed the following:

1. *Women in Sports: Horseback Riding* by Flora Golden, Harvey House, 1978
2. *Breakthrough: Women in Religion* by Betsy C. Smith, Walker, 1978
3. *Women Lawyers at Work* by Elinor P. Swiger, Messner, 1978.

4. *Legendary Women of the West* by Brad Williams, McKay, 1978

5. *Wild Animals, Gentle Women* by Margery Facklam, Harcourt Brace Jovanovich, 1978

In at least these two areas of nonfiction for children and young people, the publishing industry has responded specifically to the demand for representation of women in diverse roles.

Sexist and Derogatory Language

Feminist critics—and many parents and teachers—have cringed upon reading statements such as the following:

> "Aw, you're just a dumb girl," sneered Scooter.
> "Yes, a dumb girl," echoed Robert (Cleary, 1950, pp. 42-43).
> "I guess you'll go right and tell," he said. "Just like a girl, can't keep anything to herself" (Sorensen, 1956, p. 73).
> "Accept the fact that this is a man's world and learn to play the game, my sweet" (Hunt, 1966, p. 31).

Not only were these and similar comments not rare in trade and textbook stories for children, they were not often challenged by their recipients. Apparently most characters, and by implication most authors, believed that putting down females was perfectly acceptable.

Although no systematic study of sexist comments has been conducted, to my knowledge, this type of language appears to have been reduced significantly. In the many recently published books and reading texts that I have read during the past several years, I have found few such instances. In most cases, the putdown is refuted, with logical argument or lack of credibility countering the character who makes the offending remarks. For example, in *Bridge to Terabithia* (Paterson, 1977), the following exchange appears:

> "Next thing," he said, his voice dripping with sarcasm, "next thing you're gonna want to let some *girl* run." Jess's face went hot. "Sure," he said recklessly. "Why not?" (Paterson, 1977, p. 26).

And after Leslie has won one race and the antagonist attempts to intimidate her into leaving to play hopscotch with the girls, she quietly persists and Jess again insists that she be given the chance to participate:

Frasher

Gary lowered his head like a bull. "Girls aren't supposed to play on the lower field. Better get up there before one of the teachers sees you."

"I want to run," she said quietly.

"You already did."

"Whatsa matter, Fulcher?" All Jess's anger was bubbling out. He couldn't seem to stop the flow. Whatsa matter? Scared to race her?" (Paterson, 1977, p. 26).

Other Examples of Change

Modification of sex roles and representation in children's literature has been focused primarily on the area of greatest criticism—the treatment of females. However, a few authors have attempted to portray male characters in nontraditional ways. *Bridge to Terabithia* (1977) is a unique example of an honest and sensitive treatment of a male literary character who contradicts the masculine stereotype. The young male protagonist, Jess, fills many masculine roles expected by his family, but the story focuses on his relationship with a young girl, his artistic inclinations, and his sensitivity—in other words, his differentness. Initially frustrated at being defeated by the girl in a race, Jess overcomes his negative feelings and finds that he and Leslie have many mutual interests and that he can learn from her as well as help her adjust to her new environment. When she dies in a tragic accident, Jess also learns to express his grief. Jess is one of the most satisfactorily developed nontraditional male main characters in books for children.

Zolotow's *William's Doll* (1972) was one of the first and is probably the best known picture book of this type. Zolotow's *A Father Like That* (1972) and *A Summer Night* (1974) also portray males with nontraditional personal characteristics. Another popular picture book is *Max* (Isadora, 1976), which is about a little boy who warms up for baseball by attending ballet class with his sister.

In contrast to Jess (*Bridge to Terabithia*), the interests in feminine concerns that Max and William show appear to be somewhat contrived. The authors of both of these picture books make it clear that the boys are adding a feminine type of behavior to well integrated masculine personalities. Both books make an important point, but it is carefully couched in traditional sex typed contexts.

Near didacticism is not limited to attempts to broaden male literary roles. Two publishers, The Feminist Press and Lollipop Power, have made noble attempts to portray females in nonstereotyped, nontraditional roles and settings. Unfortunately, these books are too frequently contrived and obvious; too often they also fall short of literary merit (e.g. *The Dragon and the Doctor*, Danish, 1971; *The Sheep Book*, Goodyear, 1972; *Exactly Like Me*, Phillips, 1972). Equally unfortunate was the attempt by Isabella Taves to recount the fictionalized account of the treatment of a little girl who dared to play in an all male Little League (*Not Bad for a Girl*, 1972). Told from an adult perspective, with little attempt at realistic development of the character of the girl in question, the book does not succeed as a story for children. Thus, the rush to respond to elements of feminist criticism resulted in too many examples of marginal or poor literature.

Summary and Conclusions

In summary, in response to the question of whether and how sex roles have changed in books for children, it is possible to infer some trends and make a few generalizations:

1. Progress has been made in the area of fiction for children in terms of increasing the number of females in main character roles and in portraying them with more positive and varied personality characteristics and in a greater variety of behaviors. This appears to be particularly true with respect to books for children in middle and late childhood years.
2. Derogatory statements about females have almost disappeared in books for children. When they appear, they are countered by factual and logical arguments in realistic contexts.
3. Picture books appear to remain largely stereotyped, although notable exceptions have been observed by this author and appear in bibliographies of nonsexist books (Adell and Klein, 1976; Bissett, 1979).
4. Special purpose books designed to compensate for the absence of women in varied occupational roles have

appeared in increasing numbers.

5. Didacticism is present in varying degrees.

Although it is clear that sex role stereotypes have not been eliminated in children's literature during the past decade, it is evident that both quantitative and qualitative improvements have been made in the treatment of females. Although optimism is appropriate at this point, complacency is not. The very fact that females are treated separately in career education books and collective biographies instead of integrated fully into books about occupations emphasizes the unusualness of seeing women in varied roles. Until more authors are able to write with ease about both sexes engaged in a broad scope of activities and exhibiting a broad range of characteristics, the children's book field as a whole will remain stereotyped. The number of books accessible to children is immense; it will take many years of publishing quality nonsexist literature to insure that a random selection is as likely to be nonstereotyped as it is to be stereotyped.

References
Professional Books

Adell, J., & H.D. Klein. *A guide to nonsexist children's books.* Chicago: Academy Press Limited, 1976.

Association for Supervision and Curriculum Development. Resolution #8: Women and minority groups in instructional materials. Anaheim, California, 1974.

Bissett, D.J. *Toward a more positive female image: Books in picture book format.* Detroit: Wayne State University Children's Literature Center, 1979.

Britton, G.E., and M.C. Lumpkin. For sale: Subliminal bias in textbooks. *Reading Teacher,* 31 (1977), 40-45.

Children's catalog: 1969 supplement. New York: H.W. Wilson, 1969.

Children's catalog: 1979 supplement. New York: H.W. Wilson, 1979.

DeBoard, D., et al. *Guidelines to promote the awareness of human potential.* Philadelphia: J.B. Lippincott, 1975.

Feminists on Children's Literature. A feminist look at children's books. *School Library Journal,* 18 (1971), 19-24.

Frasher, R., and A. Walker. Sex roles in early reading textbooks. *Reading Teacher,* 25 (1972), 741-749.

Ginn. *Treatment of women and minority groups.* New York, 1975.

Glazer, J.I., and G. Williams. *Introduction to children's literature.* New York: McGraw-Hill, 1979.

Holt, Rinehart and Winston. *Guidelines for the development of elementary and secondary instructional materials: The treatment of sex roles.* New York, 1975.

Houghton Mifflin. *Avoiding stereotypes.* Boston, 1975.

Huck, C. *Children's literature in the elementary school.* New York: Holt, Rinehart and Winston, 1979.

International Reading Association. Committee on Sexism and Reading. Guide for evaluating sex stereotyping in reading materials. *Reading Teacher*, 31 (1977), 288-289.

Junior high school library catalog: 1979 supplement. New York: H.W. Wilson, 1979.

Key, M.R. The role of male and female in children's books—dispelling all doubt. *Wilson Library Bulletin, 46* (1971), 167-176.

Longnoin, B., and J. Garcia. Publishers respond to criticism concerning sexism in readers: But where are we now? Unpublished manuscript. San Marcos, Texas: Southwest Texas State University, n.d.

National Council of Teachers of English. New NCTE guidelines encourage nonsexist use of language. *Language Arts*, 53 (1976), 329-335.

National Education Association. *Sex role stereotyping.* Washington, D.C.: NEA, 1973.

Noyce, R.M. *Equality of the sexes in new children's fiction.* Report prepared at the University of Kansas, 1976. ED 137 802

Oliver, L. Women in aprons: The female stereotype in children's readers. *Elementary School Journal, 74* (1974), 253-259.

Rudman, M.K. *Children's literature: An issues approach.* Lexington, Massachusetts: D.C. Heath, 1976.

Sadker, M.P., and D.M. Sadker. *Now upon a time: A contemporary view of children's literature.* New York: Harper and Row, 1977.

Sexism in Textbooks Committee. *Guidelines for improving the image of women in textbooks.* Glenview, Illinois: Scott, Foresman, 1972.

Stewig, J.W., M.L. Knipfel. Sexism in picture books: What progress? *Elementary School Journal*, 76 (1975), 151-155.

Stewig, J.W., and M. Higgs. Girls grow up to be mommies: A study of sexism in children's literature. *School Library Journal*, 98 (1973), 236-241.

Taylor, M.W. Sex role stereotypes in children's readers. *Elementary English*, 50 (1973), 1045-1047.

Tiedt, I. *Exploring books with children.* Boston: Houghton Mifflin, 1979.

Weitzman, L.J., et al. Sex role socialization in picture books for preschool children. *American Journal of Sociology*, 77 (1972), 1125-1150.

Weitzman, L.J., and D. Rizzo. Sex bias in textbooks. *Today's Education*, 64 (1975), 49, 52.

Women on Words and Images. *Dick and Jane as victims: Sex stereotyping in children's readers.* Princeton, New Jersey: National Organization for Women, 1972.

Zimet, S.G. The messages in elementary reading texts. *Today's Education*, 62 (1973), 43, 60-62.

References
Children's Books

Aardema, V. *Why mosquitoes buzz in people's ears.* New York: Dial, 1975.

Blos, J.W. *A gathering of days: A New England girl's journal, 1830-1832.* New York: Charles Scribner's Sons, 1979.

Byars, B. *Summer of the swans.* New York: Viking, 1970.

Choosing careers and lifestyles (series). New York: Franklin Watts.

Cleary, B. *Henry Huggins.* New York: William Morrow, 1950.

Cooper, S. *The grey king.* New York; Atheneum, 1975.

Danish, B. *The dragon and the doctor.* Old Westbury, New York: Feminist Press, 1971.

English, B.L. *Women at their work.* New York: Dial, 1977.

Facklam, M. *Wild animals, gentle women.* New York: Harcourt Brace Jovanovich.

Fox, P. *The slave dancer.* Scarsdale, New York: Bradbury, 1973.

George, J.C. *Julie of the wolves.* New York: Harper and Row, 1972.

Goble, P. *The girl who loved wild horses.* Scarsdale, New York: Bradbury, 1978.
Golden, F. *Women in sports: Horseback riding.* New York: Harvey House, 1978.
Goodyear, C. *The sheep book.* Chapel Hill, North Carolina: Lollipop Power, 1972.
Haley, G.E. *A story, a story.* New York: Atheneum, 1970.
Hall, D. *Ox-cart man.* New York: Viking, 1979.
Hamilton, V. *M.C. Higgins, the great.* New York: Macmillan, 1974.
Hogrogian, N. *One fine day.* New York: Macmillan, 1974.
Hunt, I. *Up a road slowly.* Chicago: Follett, 1966.
Isadora, R. *Max.* New York: Macmillan, 1976.
Lasker, J. *Mothers can do anything.* Chicago: Albert Whitman, 1972.
McDermott, G. *Arrow to the sun.* New York: Viking, 1974.
Merriam, E. *Mommies at work.* New York: Alfred Knopf, 1961.
Mitchell, J.S. *I can be anything: Careers and colleges for young women.* College Entrance Examination Board, 1978.
Mosel, A. *The funny little woman.* New York: E.P. Dutton, 1972.
Musgrove, M. *Ashanti to Zulu: African traditions.* New York: Dial, 1976.
O'Brien, R.C. *Mrs. Frisby and the rats of NIMH.* New York: Atheneum, 1971.
Paterson, K. *Bridge to Terabithia.* New York: Thomas Y. Crowell, 1977.
Phillips, L. *Exactly like me.* Chapel Hill, North Carolina: Lollipop Power, 1972.
Raskin, E. *The westing game.* E.P. Dutton, 1978.
Rockwell, H. *My doctor.* New York: Macmillan, 1973.
Rothman, J. *I can be anything you can be.* New York: Scroll, 1978.
Smith, B.C. *Breakthrough: Women and religion.* New York: Walker, 1978.
Sorensen, V. *Miracles on Maple Hill.* New York: Harcourt Brace Jovanovich, 1956.
Spier, P. *Noah's ark.* New York: Doubleday, 1977.
Swiger, E.P. *Women lawyers at work.* New York: Julian Messner, 1978.
Taves, I. *Not bad for a girl.* New York: M. Evans, 1972.
Taylor, M. *Roll of thunder, hear my cry.* New York: Dial, 1976.
What can she be? (series) New York: Lothrop, Lee, and Shepard.
Williams, B. *Lengendary women of the west.* New York: David McKay, 1978.
Zemach, H. *Duffy and the devil.* New York: Farrar, Straus and Giroux, 1973.
Zolotow, C. *A father like that.* New York: Harper and Row, 1971.
Zolotow, C. *The summer night.* New York: Harper and Row, 1974.
Zolotow, C. *William's doll.* New York: Harper and Row, 1972.

Research On Language Differences between Males and Females

H. Thompson Fillmer

The vast multitude of forces with which we interact daily causes each of us to live in a world that is unique. The differences between our world and the worlds of others are apparent in the stimuli that command our attention and the ways that we process this stimuli.

Our language provides others with clues that help them to learn about the world in which we live. Thus, in a paper dealing with sex stereotyping it seems appropriate to investigate the language used by men and women, to discover how it differs, and to propose explanations for these differences.

Linguists theorize that thère are specific characteristics which distinquish male language from female language. These characteristics can be classified under two major headings. The first is the structure of language itself, and the second is the difference in usage between men and women.

Structure of Language

Certain aspects of the structure of the English language tend to make women invisible. Since our language is not divided into male and female with distinct conjugations and declensions like many other languages, women do not have an autonomous, independent existence in the English language: they are part of man (Thorne, 1979).

Grammar books agree that *he, his,* and *him* really mean *he* and *she, his* and *hers,* and *him* and *her. Man* implies *man* and *woman; men* implies *men* and *women.* This generic form of *man* tends to render women invisible. It is widely agreed that the general effect of this situation is accurately described by the adage "Out of sight, out of mind" (Greenberg, 1978; Walum, 1977).

In a junior high school experiment the teacher read a group of sentences containing *man* in its generic form, such as "Man is a gregarious animal" and "Man lives in shelters." Pupils were asked to draw pictures to illustrate the sentences. With one exception, all the pupils drew pictures of males. It was obvious that the word *man* was not generic for these pupils (Greenberg).

Markers

Another English form that tends to make women invisible is the use of markers to designate female gender. Neutral words that refer to both men and women are presented as applying only to men. There are sentences in school texts that refer to "Doctors and their wives," and "Officers and their ladies." When a Washington speaker recently announced that soon women would be in the space program, reporters immediately coined the term "astrowomen" as if the word astronaut were male (Greenberg).

Lexicographers tell us that the suffixes *or* and *er* mean "one who." For many people, these suffixes mean "a male who." Therefore, we use markers in the form of suffixes to designate "a female who" as in the case of aviatrix, actress, and poetess. Another common marker is the use of *lady, woman,* or *girl* as a noun adjunct as in lady doctor, woman runner, or girl reporter.

The words *man* and *woman* are used in English to connote maturity. Yet, the implication is made that females are immature and incompetent by the substitution of *ladies* or *girls* for *women.* Conversely, men are referred to as *gentlemen* only in infrequent formal situations. The term *boy* is reserved for young men and those in situations deemed inferior. Rarely, if ever, do males "go to the club with the boys" or "talk boy talk." Women of all ages are referred to as *girls*. Grown women "go out with the girls," are hired as "girl Fridays" and indulge in "girl talk" (Walum, 1977).

Descriptive Words
The availability of words to represent males and females is another form difference in language between men and women. The most authoritative source of words and word meanings—the dictionary—clearly indicates bias against women in terms of number of words available to designate women and men, and in the use of gender words in illustrative sentences.

An extensive analysis of the unabridged *Random House Dictionary* found that illustrative sentences used masculine gender words three times more often than feminine gender words. In these sentences females were most often shown in domestic contexts—mothers, wives, hostesses, cooks, and servants.

Sentences also showed men in "bad guys" roles twice as often as desirable contexts, such as business executives. However, males were cast in professions and positions of leadership more than were women (Gershuny, 1977).

An investigation of standardized tests indicated that in test batteries published by major test companies all but eight of twenty-seven batteries contained twice as many male references (Saario, Jacklin, and Tittle, 1973).

Females also tend to be invisible in text materials. Studies of basal reading series indicate that references to male adults and children occur approximately three times more than references to females. Boys are shown as aggressive and adept in problem solving. Girls are shown as passive—fantasizers and followers of boys' orders. Men are shown as leaders who engage in constructive activities; women are shown as conformists who are usually in service roles. At successive grade levels the number of females shown decreases, and the behavior of both males and females becomes increasingly stereotyped (Nilsen, 1977; Women on Words and Images, 1972). One investigation of adolescent novels found that none of the heroines portrayed had the smallest sense of destiny nor could any of them imagine themselves as autonomous beings. When they became pregnant, without exception, they had male babies (Heilbrun, 1970).

Descriptive words usually show men as strong and virile. Women are shown as weak and dependent. For instance larger animals are usually *he*, while smaller animals, nature, and boats are *she*. In short, "power" represents the masculine; "grace" and "acquiescence" represent the feminine.

Flexner observed that many types of slang words including the taboo and strongly derogatory ones referring to sex, women, work, money, whiskey, politics, transportation, and sports refer primarily to male endeavor and interest. Men tend to avoid words that sound feminine or weak (Flexner, 1960).

Because of various structural features of the English language, women tend to be ignored or grouped within the general category of men. There are many more words available to refer to men's interests and activities than to women's interests and activities. Words that are available tend to stereotype men as being in command, active and powerful. Women generally are portrayed as being subservient, passive, and weak. Illustrative sentences in dictionaries, standardized tests, textbooks, and literature generally refer to men three times more often than to women.

Sex Differences in Usage

Thus far, we have explored sexism in language that affects women. Now, we will look at sexism in the language of women. In considering this topic the reader must bear in mind that sex differences in language usage vary by community. In summarizing extensive anthropological literature on sex differences, Trugill concluded that "the larger and more inflexible the differences between social roles of men and women in a particular community, the larger and more rigid the linguistic differences tend to be" (Trugill, 1974).

Lakeoff (1975) presents nine linguistic features that are thought to characterize the language of women.

1. Women have a large stock of words related to their specific interests, generally relegated to them as women's work: magenta, shirr, dart

(in sewing), and so on.
2. "Empty" adjectives like divine, charming, cute....
3. Question intonation where we might expect declaratives: For instance, tag questions ("It's so hot, isn't it?")....
4. The use of hedges of various kinds. Women...are socialized to believe that asserting themselves strongly isn't nice or ladylike....
5. Related to this is the use of the intensive "so...." Here we have an attempt to hedge on one's strong feelings, as though to say, I feel strongly about this, but I dare not make it clear how strong....
6. Hypercorrect grammar; women are not supposed to talk rough....
7. Superpolite forms; women are supposed to speak more politely than men....Women don't use off-color or indelicate expressions; women are the experts at euphemism.
8. Women don't tell jokes....It is axiomatic in middle-class American society that, first, women can't tell jokes—they are bound to ruin the punch line, they mix up the order of things, and so on....
9. Women speak in italics, and the more ladylike and feminine you are, the more italics you are supposed to speak.

An analysis indicates that these features fall naturally into two major categories: conceptual constraints and propriety.

Conceptual Constraints

In our language women tend to use euphemistic terms to avoid aggressive or vigorous language. Where a man will accuse another of being a "damned liar," a woman will remark that the person in question told a "fib" (Jesperson, 1954).

Lakeoff explains the development of conceptual constraints by explaining that, as children, girls are encouraged to behave as "little ladies." Therefore, they are taught not to scream as vociferously as little boys and are chastized for throwing tantrums or displaying temper. High spirits are expected and rewarded in boys' behavior; docility and resignation are rewarded in girls' behavior. Correspondingly, society accepts a show of temper by a man, but discourages a similar tirade from a woman. Women are allowed to fuss and complain but only a man can bellow in rage (Lakeoff, 1973).

These linguistic expectations are borne out in a study of the dialogue of women and men in *New Yorker* cartoons and Sunday comic strips. In the 152 *New Yorker* cartoons, women used weaker, more restricted language; they used fewer exclamations and curse words, and they did not discuss topics such as finance or politics. The 56 Sunday comics confirmed these differerences (Kramer, 1973).

Oral speaking. Conceptual constraints are also demonstrated in the oral speech of women. One investigation concluded that men tend to talk as though they were bigger, and women as though they were smaller. Judges listening to the recorded speech of boys and girls between the ages of four and fourteen could reliably and validly identify the sex of the children from their voices. It was also concluded that boys had a more forceful definite rythym of speaking than did girls (Saario, Jacklin, and Tittle, 1973).

Patterns of speech used by women are those that tend to reflect submission—higher pitch, wider range of intonation, softer speech, and other forms considered polite and deferential (Sachs, Lieberman, and Erickson, 1973).

Other investigations indicate that in mixed conversation women are dominated by men. Men talk more often than women, interrupt women more than women interrupt them, and tend to speak with a greater intensity. Men also initiate conversation more often than women and tend to control the topic of the conversation (Sachs, Lieberman, and Erickson; Swacker, 1976). It has been suggested, however, that in group situations the less authoritative language used by women may be more effective in encouraging cooperation, providing support, and eliciting participation from group members who are reluctant to speak (Swacker).

Qualifiers. A special style associated with women is called the tag ending, which tends to diminish authority. The tag ending follows a statement with a question: "That game was exciting, wasn't it?" Tag endings may be used by a speaker who does not wish to make a definite statement, but prefers the listener to do so. Quite possibly, the same feelings that cause women to avoid aggressive or coarse language cause them to avoid making outright statements.

Another characteristically feminine speech style is the cause of intensifiers such as *quite, so, very,* and *such*: "He is so charming." "It was such a nice party." Also the use of certain adjectives such as *cute, divine, charming, lovely,* and *greenish* are signals that a woman is talking (Jesperson).

Men rarely use specific color words, but rather use general terms such as *red, blue, green, brown*, and *black*. Specific color words such as *mauve, beige, ecru, puce*, and *lavender* are rather clear indicators of women's speech (Key, 1972).

Propriety

Another major difference between the language of men and women is in the area of propriety. Women's language is "more proper" than that of men. In spite of all kinds of social and economic equalization of the sexes in our society, men and women still are segregated as it were in their freedom of language use. It is believed that most women eschew profanity and tough talk. These forms of speech ostensibly are confined largely to men. Such language use by women is interpreted by both men and women as crudeness or as a deliberate exaggeration in order to "prove something."

Jesperson (1954) reports that women in all cultures are shy at mentioning certain parts of the human body and natural functions by the direct and often rude denominations which men, especially young men, prefer when among themselves. Women, therefore, invent innocent and euphemistic words and phrases which sometimes come to be looked upon as plain or blunt names. Then women have to avoid these terms that they originally popularized and replace them with other words they consider decent. Women choose their words from the central field of language avoiding everything extreme or bizarre. Men often coin new words or expressions or reintroduce obsolete ones. In this way, men attempt to find more adequate or precise expressions for their thoughts.

Firestone (1970) offers an explanation for this particular difference in the language usage of men and women.

> As for the double standard about cursing: A man is allowed to blaspheme the world because it belongs to him to damn—but the same curse out of the mouth of a woman or a minor, i.e., an "incomplete man" to whom the world does not yet belong, is considered presumptuous, and thus an impropriety or worse.

Development of Sexism in Language

At birth, an infant enters one of society's first tracking systems—the sex role. If it is a male infant, his first gifts are primarily blue clothes, tools, and sports equipment to designate masculinity. His parents and their friends throw him into the air, catch him, and generally expose him to rough, aggressive activity.

If it is a female infant, she receives pink, dainty clothes to designate femininity and dolls, kitchen implements, and domestic items. Her parents handle her gently and discourage her from rough and tumble activities and language.

Infants learn early that the generic *man* and the use of markers to designate females makes the female in English relatively inconspicuous. As the infants become more proficient in language, they notice that both oral language and literary references portray men as the vigorous and dominant sex. Women speak and are spoken of as if they were docile, passive, and subsurvient to men.

These language differences affect both children's language and thinking. By three years of age children stereotype the sexes according to occupation (Greenberg). Pupils in grades one through five are able to perceive subtle differences between the language of men and women in the areas of propriety, use of tags, intensifiers, conceptual constraints, and occupational roles (Fillmer and Haswell, 1977).

When the child enters school, these same sex stereotypes are perpetuated and others are added. Children line up by sex in many schools. They learn that boys operate slide projectors and tape recorders, while girls perform housekeeping duties such as cleaning up the room and preparing decorations.

Textbooks further reinforce the notion of the inconspicuous woman. A task force of the National Organization of Women, called Women on Words and Images, conducted a two year study of sex role stereotyping in children's readers. They read 134 books from 12 different publishers and carefully documented 2,760 stories.

One of the major findings of this study was that boys and men are present in the readers in overwhelmingly larger numbers than are girls and women. The ratio of boy-centered to girl-centered stories was 5 to 2; adult male main characters to adult female main characters, 3 to 1; male biographies to female biographies, 6 to 1; male animal stories to female animal stories, 2 to 1; and male folk or fantasies to female folk or fantasies, 4 to 1.

In the general area of restraints this study indicated that clever girls appeared 33 times, clever boys 131; girls solved problems 47 times, boys 169; adventuresome, imaginative girls appeared 68 times, boys 216; yet, passive and dependent girls appeared 119 times, boys 19.

Although children already stereotype occupations, these same stereotypes are strengthened in elementary school readers. The readers offered 26 traditional career opportunities for women compared to 147 for men. Job holders were rarely mothers. The 134 books surveyed contained three with working mothers. As the authors note:

> A young girl is constantly being "sold" on nursing over doctoring, stenography over business...and on motherhood over other alternatives. The little lamb asks her mother what she can be, and the Mother says: "You can be a sheep. A mother sheep, just like me." The message is rarely this explicit; it doesn't have to be (Women on Words and Images, 1972).

Research evidence indicates that by the time a child completes elementary school, he has averaged more than 20,000 hours viewing TV. Here, too, sex stereotypes are inflicted upon the viewer. Women continue to be intellectually inferior housewives who are overwhelmed by the smooth-talking male laundry soap salesperson, the butts of some humorous situation, or inept meddlers in men's affairs. Children's programs tend to present men and boys as adventurers with girls and women in subservient roles. Bergman found that even such carefully produced programs as "Sesame Street" still stereotype female characters. Females are not presumed to be active or to be problem solvers; they provide emotional support for males, but the only tasks they perform are cleaning house and cooking, which are sometimes the subjects of instruction in such programs (Berman, 1972).

Conclusions

Sex stereotyping does not result from a single cause. Everything that affects the behavior of an individual affects the language of that individual.

A portion of sex stereotyping results from the characteristics of our language. Efforts are being made to reduce the use of the generic *man* and feminine markers.

Feminine use of language is another form of sex stereotyping. Efforts are underway by many feminist organizations to raise the consciousness of women so that they will eliminate the use of hedges, empty adjectives, tags, and super correct and polite language.

Parents and teachers of young children must establish environments free from sex bias. Girls must have more freedom in physical activities and fewer career limitations. Boys must have more freedom in expressing emotions and sharing responsibilities with girls.

Publishers must follow guidelines designed to reduce the stereotypes of women as sex objects and passive observers of life with career potential only as secretaries, nurses, teachers, or clerks. School textbooks should include an equal number of references to women and men. Both women and men should be shown as athletes, leaders, and with equal degrees of competence. Women should also be entitled to share the role of villain along with her male counterparts.

The media must continue to employ women for high level positions such as editors, TV newspersons, hosts, and interviewers. Programs and articles should include more women as subjects. TV commercials must stop depicting women as mindless victims of smooth-talking male salespersons or hapless bunglers in problem solving situations. At present, TV commercials are the worst offenders in presenting derogatory images of women.

Space does not permit analyses of the affects of such important issues as politics, religion, the changing family, laws, and economics on linguistic sex stereotyping, but the issues that have been treated should provide the reader with an idea of the scope and seriousness of the problem.

Language influences and is influenced by our behavior. Whenever we use language that stereotypes ourselves or others into roles that are restrictive and/or inaccurate, we are engaging in an activity counterproductive to human development. Since schools are committed to maximum development of human potential, it behooves educators to investigate further the causes of sex stereotyping in language. When the causes are known, means will be available for experimental programs designed to reduce the language differences between male and female usage and to discourage the use of restrictive and inhibiting stereotypic expressions.

References

Bergman, Jane. Are little girls being harmed by Sesame Street? *New York Times*, January 2, 1972.

Fillmer, H.T., and Leslie Haswell. Sex role stereotyping in English usage. *Sex Roles, 3* (1977), 257-263.

Firestone, S. *The dialect of sex.* New York: William Morrow, 1970.

Flexner, S.B. *Dictionary of American slang.* New York: Thomas Y. Crowell, 1960.

Greenberg, Selma. *Right from the start.* Boston: Houghton Mifflin, 1978.

Gershuny, H. Lee. Sexism in dictionaries and texts: Omissions and commissions. In Alleen Pace Nilsen et al., *Sexism and language.* Urbana, Illinois: National Council of Teachers of English, 1977.

Heilbrun, Carolyn G. All pregnant girls have baby boys. *New York Times Book Review*, Part 2, November 8, 1970.

Jesperson, Otto. *Language: Its nature, development, and origin.* London: George Allen and Unwin, 1954.

Key, Mary Ritchie. Linguistic behavior of male and female. *Linguistics*, 88 (1972), 15-31.

Kramer, Cheris. Women's rhetoric in *New Yorker* cartoons: Patterns for a Mildred Milquetoast. Paper presented at the Annual Convention of the Speech Comunications Association, New York, 1973.

Lakeoff, Robin. Language and women's place. *Language in Society, 2* (1973), 45-80.

Lakeoff, Robin. *Language and women's place.* New York: Harper and Row, 1975.

Nilsen, Alleen Pace. Sexism in children's books and elementary teaching materials. In Alleen Pace Nilsen, et al., *Sexism and language.* Urbana, Illinois: National Council of Teachers of English, 1977.

Saario, Terry N., Carol Nagy Jacklin, and Carol Kehr Tittle. Sex role stereotyping in the public schools. *Harvard Educational Review,* 43 (August 1973), 386-416.

Sachs, Jacqueline, Philip Lieberman, and Donna Erickson. Anatomical and cultural determinants of male and female speech. In Roger W. Shuy and Ralph W. Fasold (Eds.), *Language attitudes: Current trends and prospects.* Washington, D.C.: Georgetown University Press, 1973.

Swacker, Marjorie. Sexistizing and desexistizing through language. *Humanist Educator*, 15 (June 1976), 171-178.

Thorne, Barrie. Claiming verbal space: Women, speech, and language in college classrooms. Paper presented at the Research Conference on Educational Environments and the Undergraduate Woman, Wellesley College, September 1979.

Trugill, P. *Sociolinguistics.* Baltimore: Penguin, 1974.

Walum, Laurel Richardson. *The dynamics of sex and gender: A sociological perspective.* Chicago: Rand McNally, 1977.

Woman on Words and Images. *Dick and Jane as victims: Sex stereotyping in children's readers.* Princeton, New Jersey: 1972.

Part Three
Instructional Strategies

The Nonsexist Classroom:
A Process Approach
Barbara Porro

Sex equity has become one of today's most important educational issues, a circumstance that is largely the result of Title IX of the Education Amendments of 1972, which prohibits sex discrimination in the schools. Although many teachers recognize and disapprove of the damaging effects of sex role stereotyping, they are at a loss about how to act to eliminate sexism effectively from their classrooms.

A nonsexist classroom focuses upon helping children develop to their fullest potential as individuals rather than channeling them into behaviors and interests dictated by a cultural stereotype. Boys and girls are given equal opportunities to explore a variety of skills and behaviors.Children are taught to recognize and appreciate individual differences in others without regard to sex. Friendships across sex lines are encouraged. Children are also assisted in overcoming limitations of their previous sex role identification. Girls are taught the importance of developing strong, well-coordinated bodies and boys are given the opportunity to express their emotions. By developing a wider range of human emotions and role skills, children cope more effectively with the complexities of today's world.

In an effort to develop teacher techniques for eliminating sex bias from the classroom, a research project was designed and implemented in my first grade classroom. The study measured the effects of a nonsexist classroom upon the sex role attitudes of first graders. The author developed the "Sex Role Attitude Inventory" after that of Flerx, Fidler, and Rogers (1976), to use as a pre and posttest to measure attitudinal change. The study compared a nonsexist classroom with two control first grade classrooms. (A monograph reporting the results of the study is available from P.K. Yonge Laboratory School.) The purpose of this discussion is to describe the method developed in the study for eliminating sex bias from the classroom. This experience may serve as a model for other teachers working toward the same goal.

Development of the Method

The method used in creating the nonsexist classroom can best be described as a process approach developed in response to daily classroom experiences. As an initial step, the classroom environment was modified to support a nonsexist perspective. The physical layout was rearranged by combining block and house areas, and art and carpentry areas. Whenever possible, instruction was tailored to meet the needs of the individual. Differences in individual student learning styles, interests, and abilities were taken into consideration. For example, the children were grouped by ability for phonics instruction, but they read aloud individually for their reading lesson. The children chose their readers from a variety of books available on their level. As students progressed through self-selected material at their own pace, their feeling of success with reading was insured.

Since research indicates that teachers treat boys and girls differently, it was important that the teacher become aware of her own sexist behavior and interaction patterns with children. Boys, for example, typically receive more positive and more negative attention than do girls (Meyer and Thompson, 1956). The teacher was also careful to use nonsexist language and to model nonstereotypic behavior. For example, a female teacher can operate a film projector as competently as a male teacher.

The children's responses to the modified environment were favorable; they were cooperative and willingly accepted the new arrangement. Several weeks into the study, however, it became obvious that no change was occurring in their attitudes or behaviors. Even when given a choice, they continued to act out sex typed roles. The modifications in the environment were not enough to create behavioral change. The change had to occur in the children themselves because they already had been trained to perform sex stereotyped behavior long before entering the classroom. It would take a more radical approach to neutralize these deeply socialized patterns.

The teacher developed a new strategy, this time taking cues from the children. First, sexist attitudes and behaviors among the children were examined and defined. Each problem was discussed with the children to identify the reasons behind their behavior. New classroom values that supported specific nonsexist behaviors were established. And finally, the children participated in activities that provided them with opportunities to experience new, nonsexist ways of behaving. This confrontative approach required active intervention on the part of the teacher. The teacher had to participate with a high level of commitment in order to create the opportunities for change.

One of the most obvious problems was the fact that boys and girls automatically segregated themselves at play time and often expressed negative attitudes toward the opposite sex group. In their study, Bianchi and Bakeman (1978) used same sex affiliation as an index of the degree to which children perceived conventional behavior as appropriate. Guttentag and Bray (1976) reported that the less familiar an individual is with another group, the more easily that group is described in stereotypical terms. They concluded that "increased interaction between boys and girls is one effective means of erasing the limitations that each sex imposes on the other" (p. 300).

The environment had already been modified to support cross sex affiliation. Children of both sexes were integrated whenever possible so that they had natural opportunities to experience each other in daily living and learning situations. Seating arrangements, lining up, small group instruction, and games involving teams were all sexually integrated. These subtle modifications in organizational patterns, however, were not enough to change the often antagonistic behavior between boys and girls. Although they were compelled to interact more often, they continued to interact in the same hostile ways.

Instructional Strategies

Story time had always been a natural focal point for exploring the complexities of the human experience and for establishing classroom values and codes of acceptable behavior. Story time, therefore, became a good vehicle for promoting the idea that boys and girls can play together. Over a period of a week, stories of boys and girls approaching each other, playing together, and making friends were read and discussed (Hoban, 1969; Iwasaki, 1970; Udry, 1965). The children's reactions were predictable. Some were disgusted: "Yuk! Girls/Boys!" Some were proud to announce that they already had friends of the opposite sex, and others remained quiet and uncommitted. In the heated discussions that followed, many sexist taboos were revealed; girls and boys who played together were viewed as "tomboys," "sissies," or "in love."

As teacher and children explored these loaded words together, the unfairness of such labeling was emphasized. Children began to admit that it was possible for boys and girls to play together just because they liked each other. The stories and the talks helped to establish a new classroom value: Boys and girls can be friends.

In spite of this supportive environment, the majority of the class did not magically cross the girl-boy line and begin socializing. The teacher had to assume an active role in introducing children to new ways of interacting. A New Friends Game was designed specifically for this purpose. At play time, individuals were taken aside and asked to name children in the class they would like to have as new friends. Boys and girls named each other more freely in this private interview than they might have publicly. Using this list of names, two or three children were matched together and assigned a task, such as playing checkers or erecting a hospital with big building blocks. The object of the game was to complete the task and make a new friend. Making it a compulsory, timed activity diverted the children's attention from the fact that they were interacting with new playmates. The first time they played this game, the children were assembled afterward and they talked about their experiences. One of the ideas reinforced in the discussion was that many boys and girls had played together and become friends.

Porro

The class continued to play the New Friends Game once a week. Before each game the children were given an opportunity to revise their list of potential friends. Not only did boys and girls begin naming each other more frequently, but they began socializing outside the context of the game—sitting together at group meetings, lunch time, and work time. Any new friendships that became visible were encouraged and supported: "Jessica, are you and Jason new friends? That's great!" At the end of several weeks, all the children demonstrated awareness of the possibility of having friends of the opposite sex, and many had experienced it and valued it for themselves.

This first strategy successfully completed, another sexist behavior was identified to focus upon. Many girls spent their play time in the classroom playing house, caring for their dolls, and arranging their hair before a mirror. Although there is value in this type of imitative play, the girls were missing important opportunities for physical exercise and for participation in team activities where valuable group procedures were being learned. Jenkins and MacDonald (1979, p. 20) reported that girls are inhibited in active play because of cultural signals that reinforce concern with their appearance, neatness, and cleanliness. It seems necessary to teach the girls that physical fitness and athletic ability are desirable characteristics for girls as well as boys.

Creating an awarenesss and appreciation for body fitness and strength began with a guest athlete who came to the classroom dressed in jogging clothes. She talked to the children about how muscles function and how they are developed. She showed them her muscles, and they showed her their muscles. She specifically stressed the idea that it is important for everyone to keep physically fit. She led the class in several exercises and talked about the many ways they could work to develop strong bodies.

Physical fitness thus established as a new classroom value, the teacher announced she would spend part of play time actively participating outside. Here the teacher's role modeling behavior was used as an effective strategy. The girls in the playhouse left their dolls and followed her out to the playground. They climbed on the jungle gym, crawled through the pipes, and played follow-the leader. Much of the fun, however, seemed to be happening on the soccer field, where the boys spent most of their free time running and kicking. In a natural progression of events, the strategy aimed at making physical activity attractive to the girls led to an ideal opportunity to involve both sexes in a team activity. At the teacher's suggestion, the girls asked the boys if they could join the game. The boys had no objection: "Sure, you can play! Let's choose sides again."

When the girls joined the game, a new problem emerged. The girls clustered together on the field, hands behind their backs, and watched the action around them. Playing soccer was a skill they had not yet acquired. It was necessary for the female teacher to act as a model. As she ran, kicked, and followed the action, so did the girls. After several weeks of coaching, some of the girls became sufficiently skilled to enjoy the game and be valuable team members.

There are still girls (and now boys) who sometimes stay inside and play house during their play time. The difference now is that they have consciously chosen that activity from a variety of options, many of which they have experienced firsthand.

The soccer experience illustrates the cumulative effect of the process approach. Once a new value became internalized, the children were increasingly more receptive to other new ideas, and the process of change was facilitated. The girls' easy entry into a previously all-boy activity was a direct result of the new value established in the New Friends Game.

The children had many sexist attitudes about future adult roles. Several units of study, centering around careers, parenting, and home management, were developed to modify these attitudes. Children's books were used to introduce the children to the main ideas of each unit. Instruction was followed by direct experiences utilizing guest speakers and/or field trips. In learning about parenting, for instance, the class first read and discussed several children's books dealing with child care (Andry and Kratka, 1970; Byars, 1971; Zolotow, 1972). The mothers and fathers came to the classroom with their babies and showed the children how to diaper, clothe, feed, and love the baby. Before they could practice these skills on the dolls in the classroom, however, the taboo prohibiting boys from playing with dolls had to be eliminated. This was accomplished not only by inviting fathers and older brothers to demonstrate child care skills, but through many intensive discussions in which boys were regularly reassured that they could play with dolls in the classroom without being teased. Teasers, rather than those who played with dolls, were made the outsiders. The new classroom value established was that playing with dolls helps to prepare everyone for parenthood. Once they felt safe from peer ridicule, boys were enthusiastic about practicing child care through doll play.

As the nonsexist classroom opened up new options for boys and girls, it became necessary to confront the sexist ideas that constantly appeared in the everyday environment. Terms that a six-year-old could easily understand had to be used to discuss sexism with the children. One of the most useful phrases for labeling sexist ideas was "old-fashioned"; for example, "People used to think that men could not be nurses. Now we know that's an old-fashioned idea."

Children's books often provided an excellent opportunity to apply sharpened awareness because many of these books employ sexist concepts in both text and illustrations. The children enjoyed being detectives and ferreting out old-fashioned ideas: "Look, this book is old-fashioned. It says that nurses wear dresses" (obviously a half-truth, since a male nurse and a female nurse had visited the classroom, and neither of them had been wearing a dress). Inconsistencies, errors, and chauvinistic attitudes—whether discovered by the children or pointed out by the teacher—stimulated many consciousness raising discussions. The children decided how the words or pictures could be changed to reflect a more realistic view of the world. Some books underwent only minor revisions: "fireman" and "policeman," for instance were changed to "firefighter" and "police officer." In stories where girls were completely left out of the action, the children suggested that a girl's name be substituted for one of the boy main characters. At times it was necessary to revise an entire paragraph. For example, when girls and boys exhibited hostility toward each other the children noted that the boys and girls in that story had not yet learned they could be friends. A few stories were so blatantly sexist that the children wrote letters to the author recommending changes.

In a similar manner, nonsexist children's books were brought into the classroom to reinforce new ways of thinking. Books that offered children the widest range of choices were recognized and appreciated as valuable representations of the world as they now perceived it.

By the end of the experiment, the nonsexist curriculum could not be separated from the basic first grade curriculum. The process of perceiving sexism in the classroom and actively dealing with it was as natural for the teacher as diagnosing and remediating reading errors. Each time a sexist idea was confronted, the nonsexist values were strengthened. Through consistent reinforcement of nonsexist ideas, they continually validated their experience and created an environment free from sex stereotypes.

Process Model for Change

The process used in eliminating sexism from this experimental classroom does not lend itself to simple linear description. There are, however, key steps which can be identified and charted to help illuminate the basic design (see Figure 1). The teacher should keep in mind that the steps may overlap and their sequence may vary.

1. *Develop awareness.* Teachers must develop their awareness of sexism as it exists within themselves, their classrooms, and the world around them.

2. *Lay the foundation.* Modify the environment to support a nonsexist perspective. Physical layout, curriculum instructional materials, organizational techniques, and inter-action patterns are made consistent with nonsexist priorities.

3. *Conceptualize the problem.* Identify and examine sexist attitudes and behaviors among the students.

4. *Treat the problem.*

   a. Choose one sexist behavior/attitude as a problem on which to focus. Challenge the students' thinking by introducing the corresponding nonsexist attitude.

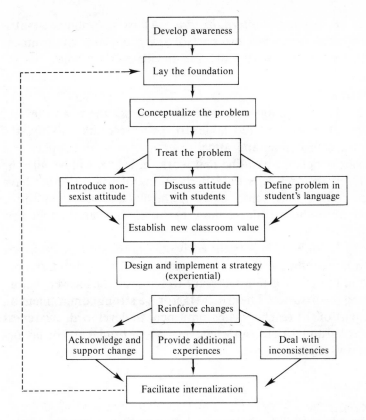

Figure 1. Flow chart of the key steps in the process approach.

      b. Discuss the problem with the students. Give them an opportunity to define the problem in their own terms.
      c. Establish the new (nonsexist) classroom value.
      d. Design and implement a strategy for change. Create an opportunity for the students to *experience* the nonsexist behavior.
    5. *Reinforce changes.* Acknowledge and support the change as it occurs. Provide students with additional experiences or repeat the initial strategy. Expose any inconsistencies that appear in the environment (books, instructional materials, attitudes) by discussing them together, using a critical eye.

6. *Facilitate internalization.* Allow the nonsexist attitude/behavior to become part of the classroom environment both for the individual child and the class as a whole.

Summary

In designing nonsexist classrooms, there are several excellent resources available to help teachers modify the physical, academic, and affective environment in support of a nonsexist perspective. The real work, however, will be with the children themselves, whose perceptions of role behavior have been defined long before entering the classroom. It is up to the teacher to show children how to think, feel, and act in new nonsexist ways.

In looking back to the early days of the study, I am struck with how unprepared I was to combat sexism in the classroom and in myself. It is not necessary to know all the answers before taking the first step. The critical factor is a strong commitment on the part of the teacher—a commitment to develop an awareness of sexism and to confront whatever sexist attitudes and behaviors that awareness reveals.

References

Andry, A.C., and S.C. Kratka. *Hi, new baby.* New York: Simon and Shuster, 1970.

Bianchi, B., and R. Bakeman. Sex typed affiliation preferences observed in preschoolers: Traditional and open school differences. *Child Development,* 49 (1978), 910-912.

Byars, B. *Go and hush the baby.* New York: Viking, 1971.

Flerx, C., D. Fidler, and R. Rogers. Sex role stereotypes: Developmental aspects and early intervention. *Child Development,* 47 (1976), 998-1007.

Guttentag, M., and H. Bray. *Undoing sex stereotypes.* New York: McGraw-Hill, 1976.

Hoban, R. *Best friends for Frances.* New York: Harper and Row, 1969.

Iwasaki, C. *Will you be my friend?* New York: McGraw-Hill, 1970.

Jenkins, J.K., and P. MacDonald. *Growing up equal.* Englewood Cliffs, New Jersey: Prentice-Hall, 1979.

Meyer, W.J., and G.G. Thompson. Sex differences in the distribution of teacher approval and disapproval among sixth graders. *Journal of Educational Psychology,* 47 (1956), 385-396.

Porro, B. *Nonsexist elementary education: A research report and teacher's guide,* research monograph # 34. Gainesville: University of Florida, P.K. Yonge Laboratory School, 1981.

Udry, J.M. *Next door to Laura Linda.* Chicago: Albert Whitman, 1965.

Zolotow, C. *William's doll.* New York: Harper and Row, 1972.

Resources for Teachers

Greenberg, S. *Right from the start: A guide to nonsexist child rearing.* Boston: Houghton Mifflin, 1979.

Guttentag, M., and H. Bray. *Undoing sex stereotypes.* New York: McGraw-Hill, 1976.

Jenkins, J.K., and P. MacDonald. *Growing up equal.* Englewood Cliffs, New Jersey: Prentice-Hall, 1979.

Johnson, L.O. (Ed.). *Nonsexist curricular materials for elementary schools.* Old Westbury, New York: Feminist Press, 1974. (Box 334, zip 11568)

Shargel, S., and I. Kane. *We can change it!* San Francisco: Change for Children, 1974. (2588 Mission Street, zip 94110)

Sprung, B. *Nonsexist education for young children: A practical guide.* New York: Citation Press, 1975.

Multicultural Nonsexist Education: A Two Edged Sword

Nora Lee Hoover

Teachers in today's schools are being urged to create learning environments that are nonsexist and multicultural. These educational goals, reflecting societal changes relating to the women's movement and to reawakened interest in ethnic roots, are viewed by some as being complementary or even identical. However, the classroom teacher who attempts to promote cultural pluralism within the context of a truly nonsexist classroom may find the mesh somewhat more difficult to achieve in practice than in theory. Part of the problem has to do with the goals of education that are multicultural; part with the materials that are frequently used.

Goals and Materials: Potential Sources of Conflict

Although the objective of some multicultural programs may be limited to increasing student awareness of cultural differences, in many cases the goal is not simply an appreciation of differences but, rather, an acceptance and an affirmation of various ethnic lifestyles including patterns of speech, mores, values, and customs (Banks, 1973). These lifestyles are depicted largely through printed and audiovisual material describing the experiences of individuals in the ethnic group under study. To be sure, multicultural education encompasses more than curricular materials, but often the main vehicle for attempting to achieve an understanding of ethnic groups is to require students to read about them. Unfortunately, students often encounter stereotypic portrayals of the sexes in materials which are considered accurate case studies of minority lifestyles.

Not too long ago, I was attempting to describe to a colleague this potential source of conflict between multicultural and nonsexist education. His response was to hand me a book saying, "Read this and then tell me if you still feel the same way." The book was *In Praise of Diversity: A Resource Book for Multicultural Education* (Gold, Grant, and Rivlin, 1977). On page 15 I came across this observation:

> We can smile tolerantly at the ten year old boy who says, "Girls are all alike," and decides not to have anything to do with any of them from now on. We know that he will change his mind and act differently as he matures. We cannot afford, however, to be equally unmoved by teachers who say, "All Blacks are alike," or "All Chicanos are alike."

The author offers no evidence in support of his assertion that ten year old boys outgrow sexist attitudes as they mature. On the contrary, common sense and experience suggest that many do not. The insinuation here that sexism is tolerable in the school setting whereas racism is not is disturbing in its implications for equality of education opportunity. This single quote, while not representative of the philosophy in the volume as a whole, does serve to illustrate that some educators who promote multi-culturalism as a means of eliminating racism are not as aware of the long range effects of sexism.

The results of this failure to consider both forms of prejudice as equally damaging can be seen in classroom practices. Teachers attempting to implement a culturally pluralistic approach, for example, may teach a two week unit on "The Changing Role of Women in American Society" with much of the remainder of the multicultural curriculum devoted to the indirect reinforcement of sexual stereotypes via materials describing cultures that are clearly sexist in their treatment of women. In this situation, the teacher is in the curious position of providing students with materials that exhibit the same type of sex stereotyping currently being removed from most reading series. The purpose of providing such case studies of ethnic life is the development of sensitivity and tolerance, if not acceptance.

The challenge for the classroom teacher is one of guiding students to an understanding of cultural differences while at the same time enabling them to arrive at their own independent judgments regarding sex roles and other aspects of lifestyle among cultural groups under study.

Recognizing Sexism in Multicultural Materials: Strategies

The first step for teachers attempting to implement a culturally pluralistic approach in a nonsexist context is to be aware of the inherent conflict between the values they are projecting in the classroom and those exemplified by ethnic groups included in the multicultural curriculum. The second step is to design lessons so that, in becoming aware of this conflict, students will experience intellectual, social, and emotional growth.

The particular skills students need if they are to process case studies of ethnic life in the manner described are the same skills demanded by most critical reading tasks: The ability to detect underlying assumptions; to differentiate fact from opinion; to determine cause and effect relationships; to infer the author's point of view and evaluate worth, desirability, and appropriateness. Development of these thinking/reading skills may be achieved through a directed reading approach, an instructional framework, an advance organizer, or any other lesson structure a classroom teacher routinely uses in content area reading situations.

The following pre and post discussion questions are offered by way of suggesting the type of direction teachers can provide at the middle school and secondary levels to guide students' developing awareness of and ability to deal with sex role stereotyping in multicultural materials. The questions are designed to be used with case-study descriptions of life in various cultural groups.

Critical Reading Skill

Detecting underlying
assumptions.

Differentiating fact
from opinion.

Determination of cause
and effect relationships.

Detecting point
of view.

Evaluation of worth,
desirability,
appropriateness.

Discussion Questions

- What does this culture
  view as the important
  differences between men
  and women?
- What basis does there
  seem to be for these
  perceived differences?
- Within this ethnic group,
  how much freedom do
  individuals have in
  choosing a life's work?
- How are people's choices
  constrained by the culture?
- What are the options
  available to men/women?
- How are their lives
  influenced as a result?
- Suppose this case study
  were read by three
  different people: A
  successful businessman,
  a female medical doctor,
  and a religious leader
  from within the culture
  itself. What would each
  think about the appropriateness of the sex roles in
  this ethnic group? Why?
- To what extent do people
  within this culture have
  opportunities to realize
  their full potentials as
  human beings?
- What factors hamper people
  in this cultural group

in developing their
talents and skills?

- Do the same constraints
  affect males as well as
  females?
- What are the advantages
  and disadvantages of
  being a male/female in this
  culture?

Summary

The creation of a multicultural and nonsexist learning
environment requires teaching skill of the highest order. On the
affective level, the task requires that teachers lead students
through a personal process of examining their own and other
people's notions about the most basic of human behaviors. To do
so successfully, a teacher must first be aware of the potential
conflict between the lifestyles exemplified by ethnic groups
included within the multicultural curriculum and the alternate
ideal of a nonsexist, nonracist society.

On the cognitive level, providing multicultural, nonsexist
education demands the ability to help students read and think
critically without being critical; to evaluate without being
judgmental. To do this, teachers must be able to structure lessons
to develop students' abilities to detect sexism and racism as they
are perpetuated in ethnic groups as well as to discriminate
between cultural values which are and are not consistent with
democratic ideals. Finally, students must be helped to determine
for themselves which culturally defined roles facilitate human
development and which serve to limit the achievement of
individual potential in modern American society. Few other
educational movements to date have offered as much potential
for growth as do current efforts to make schools multicultural
and nonsexist. At the same time, not many curricular reforms
have been fraught with potential danger if mishandled.

Hoover

References

Banks, James A. (Ed.). *Teaching ethnic studies: Concepts and strategies.* Washington, D.C.: National Council for the Social Studies, 1973.

Gold, Milton J., Carl A. Grant, and Harry N. Rivlin (Eds.). *In praise of diversity: A resource book for multicultural education.* Washington, D.C.: Teacher Corps, Association of Teacher Educators, 1977.

Klassen, Frank H., and Donna M. Gollnick (Eds.). *Pluralism and the American teacher: Issues and case studies.* Ethnic Heritage Center for Teacher Education of the American Association of Colleges for Teacher Education, 1977.

High School Seniors Read with a Purpose: To Spot Sex Stereotyping

Gloria R. Greenbaum

From the time that evidence of sex stereotyping in books had been demonstrated in such publications as *Dick and Jane as Victims* (1972) and *Sexism in School and Society* (1973), I had searched for a class project designed to create awareness among high school students of the impact sex stereotyping has made on them and on other youngsters in their formative years. How could students understand the influence of picture books and simple readers on their own developing minds? How could they recognize the subtle ideas which had molded their present adolescent attitudes about sex identification? It occurred to me that the answer to these questions lay in the often used educational method, "learning by doing"; the students would learn about sex stereotyping by reading with a purpose. Since they were enrolled in my senior elective course entitled, "Reading Techniques," they would be studying how to preview, spot for ideas, and read with a purpose. The following assignment fulfilled reading technique objectives as well as a social awareness objective. To complete the assignment, the following steps were required:

1. Select the books
2. Complete the attitude test on the basis of pictures and captions
3. Spot for phrases
4. Read entire text quickly
5. Write an analysis

The first step of the assignment was to select, at random from the public library, ten juvenile trade books published between 1950 and 1975. The selection criteria for these books were 1) varying reading levels—picture, easy-to-read, primary and 2) publication dates representing different time points within the twenty-five year span indicated. The public librarians had been informed that high school seniors would be using the young people's section; in addition, the full nature of the project was explained to the librarians, and their cooperation was solicited in making these students feel comfortable and free to explore the shelves. It was also requested that the librarians refrain from offering any advice about making selections.

For the second step of the assignment, an attitude test similar to one used by Fillmer (1974) was adapted for these students (Table 1). To complete this part of the assignment, the students were to preview each book by looking over its pictures and captions for one quality at a time, as listed in Table 1. Their purpose was to preview for only those specific factors.

The third part of the assignment following this previewing was to specifically spot phrases and ideas in each text which either reinforced or contradicted attitudes perceived by the students as a result of their previewing—again, spotting for one quality at a time.

For the fourth step, the students were to read the text quickly with the purpose of uncovering more subtle aspects of sex stereotyping which might have been overlooked in the pre-viewing and spotting.

In addition to careful responses to the checklist and the completion of the additional steps, a two page written analysis was required of each class member; this was to state concisely each individual's conclusion about sex stereotyping in the books previewed with substantive data from the books used. The following quotes were excerpted from these analyses. The designation male or female follows each quote to identify the sex of the student so the reader can compare their responses and insights.

It is strange that not one of the books I read had a female as a main character. In the pictures, the girls were never shown alone; there

Table 1

STUDENT CHECKLIST FOR EVALUATING PICTURE BOOKS

(Go through each book you are using for the points listed below)

Title _____

Author _____ Publication Date _____

	Male	Female
1. Main character		
2. Number of illustrations of	____	____
3. Number of times children are shown		
in active play	____	____
using initiative	____	____
independent	____	____
solving problems	____	____
receiving recognition	____	____
in quiet play	____	____
receiving help	____	____
being passive	____	____
involved in sports	____	____
fearful	____	____
helpless	____	____
inventive	____	____
4. Number of times adults are shown		
in different occupations	____	____
playing with children	____	____
taking children on outings	____	____
teaching skills	____	____
giving tenderness	____	____

Student's Name _____ Class _____

was always at least one boy in the pictures. But there were plenty of pictures of boys alone. [male]

The male main characters planned elaborate adventures and rescues. They refused to play with "silly" girls and looked down on them. [female]

Out of the ten books I have read, ten out of ten place the male and female in their stereotyped roles. I feel that the authors do this so that when young boys or girls read the books they can see how they are supposed to act. [male]

You *always* see the mother doing housework and the father coming home from work. [female]

One of the stories featured eight boys flying an airplane made of boxes, an airplane which the boys themselves created. While the boys showed great imagination with these boxes, the girls showed none. This scene is a complete put down of women and a glorification of men. [male]

> Female child characters are always playing quietly with dolls and tea sets, reading books, helping mother and, even worse, portraying witches. [female]

One can note the authenticity of student language, as well as the sincerity and originality of their interpretations, rather typical of the entire class. Because of the interest engendered by the project, the class decided to prepare a statistical breakdown of their analyses. After a review and study of their responses, the group concluded that the most valid statistic from this somewhat informal project would be the ratio of male main characters to female main characters.

The statistical breakdown reveals that 29 students read 218 different books; had title duplications been allowed, the total would have been 290 books. Table 2 indicates that of these 218 books, 160 or 75 percent centered around a male as a main character.

Table 2
ANALYSIS OF CENTRAL CHARACTER BY SEX

Number of Students Involved	Total Number Books Analyzed	Number of Books with Male Central Character	Number of Books with Female Central Character
29	218	160 (75%)	58 (25%)

In their analyses, many students remarked on this preponderance of male central characters. They also noted that the females as both central and noncentral characters were most frequently portrayed as homemakers or in "service" roles: stewardess, teacher, or nurse. An occupational exception to the service role occurred when the main female character was a witch! Most students also noted that in contrast to this limited view of women's occupations was the variety of jobs men performed and that, while girls copied their mothers, boys modeled themselves after their fathers. The ramifications of this fact, in view of the maternal, service, and housekeeping roles of women represented, were duly cited by both male and female students. Some seniors noted a change in sex stereotyping from the 1950s to the 1970s; they concluded that "women's liberation" affected the portrayal of women and girls and unanimously commended this trend whenever cited.

Several students commented on the rigid proscriptions for boys, noting that only in recent books were male youngsters shown crying or working in a kitchen. The students commented that these were laudable exceptions to the usual "boy" role which was also perceived as frequently antagonistic to females. These seniors noted that often little boys refused to play with girls or that the girls' mothers refused to allow them to play with the boys. Further, little girls who were excluded from play with boys discovered that reading alone in one's room provided great satisfaction. The obvious consequences of these sex stereotyped depictions were mentioned in many student papers.

The fact that eighteen year old students independently perceived such subtle influences demonstrates the effectiveness of this assignment. Most of the seniors commented that they had never realized children's books were doing more than telling a story. Likewise, they now better understood how their attitudes were strongly influenced by the portrayal of girls and boys, men and women, in these early childhood books. It also led them to speculate, in class discussion, about subtle influences of other reading materials. It can be seen that while this assignment was limited in scope, it proved valuable in several respects; it accomplished a humanistic goal while it pragmatically reinforced the reading skills of previewing, spotting, and reading with a purpose.

References

Dick and Jane as victims. Princeton: Women on Words and Images, 1972.

Fillmer, H. Thompson. Consciousness raising: Sexist teaching—What you can do. *Teacher*, 91 (January 1974), 30.

Frazier, Nancy, and Myra Sadker. *Sexism in school and society.* New York: Harper and Row, 1973.

Appendix

Eliminating Sex Stereotyping in the Classroom Environment: Resources for Teachers

Marguerite K. Gillis

BASIC READINGS

These books and booklets provide general background information about sexism and sex role stereotyping in American education.

American Association of School Administrators. *Sex equality in school.* Arlington, Virginia: American Association of School Administrators, 1975.

Anderson, S. *Differences and discrimination in education.* Worthington, Ohio: Charles A. Jones, 1972.

Frazier, N., and M. Sadker. *Sexism in school and society.* New York: Harper and Row, 1973.

Gough, P. *Sexism: New issue in American education.* Bloomington, Indiana: Phi Delta Kappan Educational Foundation, 1976.

Guttertag, M., and H. Bray. *Undoing sex stereotypes.* New York: McGraw-Hill, 1976.

Kampelman, M. *WEAL K-12 education kit.* Washington, D.C.: Women's Equity Action League, 1973.

Mullis, I. *Educational achievement and sex discrimination.* Denver: National Assessment of Educational Progress, 1975.

National Education Association. *Sex role stereotyping in the schools.* Washington, D.C.: National Education Association, 1977.

Sprung, B. (Ed.). *Perspectives on nonsexist early childhood education.* New York: Teachers College Press, 1978.

Stacey, J., S. Bereand, and J. Daniels. *And Jill came tumbling after: Sexism in American education.* New York: Dell, 1974.

Taylor, S. (Ed.). *The 51 percent minority.* Washington, D.C.: National Education Association, 1972.

CLASSROOM IDEAS

The following publications contain units, lesson plans, and other ideas for classroom activities to help students examine and overcome sex role stereotyping in all areas of the curriculum. In addition, many contain background information, bibliographies, resource lists, and reports of the results of the implementation of nonsexist curricula. These would be useful for pre or inservice teacher education and are marked with an asterisk.

*Association for Childhood Publications International. *Growing free.* Washington, D.C.: Association for Childhood Publications International, 1976.

*Boslick, N., P. Kaspar, and N. Sallan. *How to deal with sex role stereotyping.* Cupertino, California: Choice for Tomorrow, 1976.

*Cohen, M. *Stop sex role stereotyping in elementary education.* Hartford, Connecticut: Public Interest Research Group, 1974.

*Daitch, S., L. Lansberry, and J. Williams. *Sex role stereotypes teacher's guide.* Watertown, Massachusetts: Authors, 1975.

*Emma Willard Task Force on Education. *Sexism in education.* Minneapolis, Minnesota: Emma Willard Task Force on Education, 1972.

*Guttentag, M., and H. Bray. *Undoing sex role stereotypes.* New York: McGraw-Hill, 1976.

Highline School District. *The yellow blue and red book.* Seattle, Washington: Highline School District, 1975.

*Johnson, L. *Nonsexist curricular materials for elementary schools.* Old Westbury, New York: Clearinghouse on Women's Studies, 1977.

Moberg, V. *Consciousness raisers.* Old Westbury, New York: Feminist Press, 1972.

Morfield, S. *Nonsexist learning and teaching with young children.* Washington, D.C.: Eric Document Reproduction Service, 1978.

*Ontario Institute for Studies in Education. *The women's kit...and more.* Toronto, Ontario: Ontario Institute for Studies in Education, 1974.

Resource Center on Sex Roles in Education. *Today's changing roles.* Washington, D.C.: Resource Center on Sex Roles in Education, 1974.

Shargel, S., and I. Kane. *We can change it.* San Francisco, California: Change for Children, 1977.

Sprung, B. *Nonsexist education for young children: A practical guide.* New York: Citation Press, 1975.

*Stein, D., and others. *Thinking and doing: Overcoming sex role stereotyping in education.* Newton, Massachusetts: Educational Development Center, 1978.

Tiedt, I. *Teaching for liberation.* San Jose, California: Contemporary Press, 1975.

EDUCATING EDUCATORS

These materials are for use in helping pre and inservice teachers and administrators recognize and deal with sexism and sex role stereotyping in schools. Materials listed under Classroom Ideas, which also contain teacher education materials, are not relisted here.

American Association of School Administrators. *Sex equality in educational administration.* Arlington, Virginia: American Association of School Administrators, 1975.

Cornelia Wheadon Task Force on the Socialization of Children. *Growing up human: A four session course on sex role stereotyping.* Boston: Unitarian Universalist Women's Federation, n.d.

Froschl, M., F. Howe, and S. Kaylan. *Women's studies for teachers and administrators: A packet of inservice materials.* Old Westbury, New York: Feminist Press, 1975.

Institute for Educational Leadership. *Handbook on how to end sexism in your schools.* Washington, D.C: Institute for Educational Leadership, 1975.

Lydiard, B., and N. Miller (Eds.). *Kaleidoscope 13: What to do about 622.* Boston: Massachusetts Department of Education, Bureau of Curriculum Services, 1975.

MacEwan, P. *Liberating young children from sex roles.* Somerville, Massachusetts: New England Free Press, 1972.

Mc Cune, S., and others. *Implementing Title IX: A sample workshop.* Washington, D.C.: Resource Center on Sex Equity, 1977.

National Education Association. *Sex role stereotyping edupak.* Washington, D.C.: National Education Association, n.d.

Nickerson, E., and others. *Intervention strategies for changing sex role stereotypes: A procedural guide.* Dubuque, Iowa: Kendall/Hunt, 1975.

Resnik, G. *Challenging sex discrimination: Training modules.* Ann Arbor, Michigan: University of Michigan, 1975.

Schwartz, L. *Sex roles: Why, what, and how?* Paper presented to the American Psychological Association, Toronto, August 1978.

Verheyden-Hilliard, M. *A handbook for workshops on sex equality in education.* Washington, D.C.: American Personnel and Guidance Association, 1976.

Walker, J. *A model affirmative action plan for school and classroom practices.* New Brunswick, New Jersey: Douglass College, 1976.

PERIODICALS

Listed first are issues of professional journals devoted to sexism and sex role stereotyping in education. Periodicals from the women's movement which often deal with such topics and newsletters concerned with women and education are listed second.

Childhood Education, February 1976
Civil Rights Digest, Spring 1974
Elementary English, October 1973
Harvard Educational Review, November 1979
Harvard Educational Review, February 1980
Journal of Teacher Education, Winter 1975
Phi Delta Kappan, November 1973
School Library Journal, January 1973
School Review, February 1972
Social Studies Journal, Winter 1973
Today's Education, December 1972

E.E.O. Reporter, Madison, New Jersey
Feminist Studies, New York
Ms., Marion, Ohio
Research Action Notes, Washington, D.C.
Sex Discrimination in Education Newsletter, Ann Arbor, Michigan
Sex Roles: A Journal of Research, New York
Signs, Chicago, Illinois
Women: A Journal of Liberation, Baltimore, Maryland
Women's Studies, New York
Women's Studies Newsletter, Old Westbury, New York

REVIEWS AND SUMMARIES

These are reviews and summaries of the literature and research on sexism and sex role stereotyping in education. Books which contain such reviews and summaries are also included.

Daniels, A. *A survey of research concerns on women's issues.* Washington, D.C.: Association of American Colleges, 1975.

Frazier, N., and M. Sadker. *Sexism in school and society.* New York: Harper and Row, 1973.

Gersoni-Stavn, D. *Sexism and youth.* New York: R.R. Bowker, 1974.

Kingston, A., and T. Lovelace. Sexism and reading: A critical review of the literature. *Reading Research Quarterly*, 13 (1977), 133-161.

Levy, B. A feminist review of the literature. *Feminist Studies*, 1 (1971).

Maccoby, E., and C. Jacklin. *The psychology of sex differences.* Stanford, California: Stanford University Press, 1974.

Rosenberg, M., and L. Bergstrom. *Women and society: A critical review of the literature with a selected annotated bibliography.* Beverly Hills, California: Sage Publications, 1975.

Saario, T., C. Jacklin, and C. Tittle. Sex role stereotyping in the public schools. *Harvard Educational Review*, 43 (1973), 386-416.

Safilinos-Rothschild, C. *Sex role socialization and sex discrimination: A synthesis and critique of the literature.* Washington, D.C.: National Institute of Education, 1979.

Simpson, C. Educational materials and children's sex role concepts. *Language Arts*, 55 (1978), 161-167.

Sprung, B. (Ed.). *Perspectives on a nonsexist early childhood education.* New York: Teachers College Press, 1978.

SOME ADDRESSES

Addresses for some groups/organizations which are sources of information and help.

American Federation of Teachers, Women's Rights Committee, 1912 14 Street, Washington, D.C. 20005

Black Women's Institute, National Council of Negro Women, 1346 Connecticut Avenue, N.W., Washington, D.C. 20036

National Chicana Institute, Box 50155, Dallas, Texas 75250

NOW Legal Defense and Education Fund, Project on Equal Education Rights, 1029 Vermont Avenue, N.W., Washington, D.C. 20005

Project on the Status and Education of Women, Association of American Colleges, 1818 R. Street, N.W., Washington, D.C. 20009

Resource Center on Sex Roles in Education, National Foundation for the Improvement of Education, 1201 16 Street, N.W., Washington, D.C. 20036

Women's Action Alliance, 370 Lexington Avenue, New York, New York 19917

WEAL Education and Legal Defense Fund, 821 National Press Building, Washington, D.C. 20004

TITLE IX

These publications, by various authors, are available from the U.S. Government Printing Office.

Publication	Stock Number
Title IX: Selected Resources	017-080-01658-1
Why Title IX	017-080-01670-2
Complying with Title IX: The First	
Twelve Months	017-080-01669-9
Implementing Title IX: A Sample Workshop	017-080-01709-1
Implenting Title IX and Attaining Sex Equity:	
A Workshop Package for Elementary-Secondary	
Educators	
The Content of Title IX	017-080-01928-1
Regulation and Greivance Process	017-080-01926-4
Planning for Change	017-080-01924-8
The Administrator's Role	017-080-01932-9
The Teacher's Role	017-080-01940-0
The Community's Role	017-080-01931-1
Participant's Notebook	017-080-02006-1

Title IX of the Education Amendments of 1972 states:

No person in the United States shall, on the basis of sex, be excluded from participation in, be denied the benefits of, or be subjected to discrimination under any education program or activity receiving federal financial assistance....

IRA Guide for Evaluating
Sex Stereotyping in Reading Materials

The Committee on Sexism and Reading of the International Reading Association has developed the following checklist to assist teachers in analyzing educational materials for sex stereotypes and related language usage. All persons responsible for selecting books for classroom, school, or districtwide use or functioning in any capacity as educators should be aware of the implications of sex role stereotyping and exclusionary language.

Directions: Place a check in the appropriate space. Most items should be evaluated separately for each sex.

		Almost always	Occa- sionally	Rarely
1. Are girls and boys, men and women, consistently represented in equal balance?		___	___	___
2. Do boys and girls participate equally in both physical and intellectual activities?		___	___	___
3. Do girls and boys each receive positive recognition for their endeavors?	Females	___	___	___
	Males	___	___	___
4. Do boys and girls, fathers and mothers, participate in a wide variety of domestic chores, not only the ones traditional for their sex?	Females	___	___	___
	Males	___	___	___
5. Do both girls and boys have a variety of choices and are they encouraged to aspire to various goals, including nontraditional ones if they show such inclination?	Females	___	___	___
	Males	___	___	___
6. Are both boys and girls shown developing independent lives, independently meeting challenges, and finding their own solutions?	Females	___	___	___
	Males	___	___	___
7. Are women and men shown in a variety of occupations, including nontraditional ones? When women are portrayed as fulltime homemakers, are they depicted as competent and decisive?	Females	___	___	___
	Males	___	___	___
8. Do characters deprecate themselves because of their sex? (Example: "I'm only a girl.") Do others use denigrating language in this regard? (Example: "That's just like a woman.")	Females	___	___	___
	Males	___	___	___
9. Do the illustrations stereotype the characters, either in accordance to the dictates of the text or in contradiction to it?	Females	___	___	___
	Males	___	___	___
10. Is inclusionary language used? (For example, "police officer" instead of "policeman," "staffed by" instead of "manned by," "all students will submit the assignment," instead of "each student will submit his assignment," and so on.		___	___	___

For those who wish further guidance or information on this topic, a packet of related materials has been assembled by the Committee and is available through IRA headquarters. Write to: Stereotypes Packet, International Reading Association, 800 Barksdale Road, Box 8139, Newark, Delaware 19711, U.S.A. Enclose US$2 to cover costs.

IRA Inclusionary Language Guidelines:
Why Not Include Everyone?

Research indicates[1] that for many people the traditional use of so-called generic terms (such as "he" in reference to both women and men) is often interpreted in an exclusionary manner, suggesting a sex based limitation. Generic nouns and pronouns have been shown to be gender-specific (that is, they are often interpreted as referring only to men) or so ambiguous that the gender becomes subject to individual interpretation. At best, traditional language fails to contradict the exclusionary concept (regardless of the intent of the user), while it does serve to reinforce it.

The following guidelines were designed to encourage *inclusionary interpretations* rather than exclusionary ones. Even when published materials contain generics, the teacher can avoid them in tests and teacher-made materials.

1. Use inclusionary terms and occupational titles—for example, firefighter, police officer, cave dweller, chairperson, repair worker.
2. Use inclusionary terms for the generic "man"—for example, "human being" or "person" rather than "man," "humankind" rather than "mankind," "staffed by" rather than "manned by," "manufactured" rather than "man-made."
3. Use alternatives for the generic pronouns. There are four common ways to avoid a sentence like "A student is responsible for turning in *his* assignment."
   a. Use a substitute for the pronoun: "A student is responsible for turning in the assignment."
   b. Use plural forms: "Students are responsible for turning in their assignments."
   c. Use both pronoun forms: "A student is responsible for turning in her/his assignment."
   d. Rewrite by restructuring: "Turning in assignments is the student's responsibility."

[1]The basis for this statement includes the following:

Bem, S.L., and D.J. Bem. Does sex-biased job advertising aid and abet sex discrimination? *Journal of Applied Social Psychology,* 3 (1973), 6-18.

Harrison, L. Cro-Magnon women—in eclipse. *The Science Teacher,* 42 (1975), 8-11.

Harrison, L., and R.N. Passero. Sexism in the language of elementary school textbooks. *Science and Children,* 12 (1975), 22-25.

Kidd, V. A study of the images produced through the use of the male pronoun as the generic. *Moments in Contemporary Rhetoric and Communication,* 1 (1971), 25-29.

Schneider, J., and S. Hacker. Sex role imagery and use of the generic man in introductory texts: A case in the sociology of sociology. *American Sociologist,* 8 (1973), 12-18.

IRA Resolution on Sexism and Reading
Sexism

WHEREAS, sex stereotyping (sexism), "the practice whereby males and females are arbitrarily assigned to roles determined and limited by their sex," is harmful to the maximum growth of individuals, and

WHEREAS, society as well as individuals has much to gain from the elimination of sexism; and

WHEREAS, practices which avoid male and female stereotyping more accurately represent reality, encourage tolerance for individual differences, and allow more freedom for people to discover and express their needs, interests and abilities; therefore be it

RESOLVED THAT, the International Reading Association establish an ad hoc committee to work toward the following goals:
1. the development of an awareness among professionals about attitudes, practices, and materials relating to sexism, and
2. the promotion of such awareness among colleagues, administrators, members of boards of education and parents, and
3. the elimination of sex stereotyping.

(Date: May 1975)

IRA Resolution on the
Availability of Reading Materials

WHEREAS, the International Reading Association seeks to insure that a continuing concerted effort is made to educate teachers, students, and the general public with regard to the interaction between competing values within a society and its governmental guarantees of individual rights and freedoms, and

WHEREAS, the International Reading Association also recognizes the right and responsibility of parents to monitor the education of their children, be it

RESOLVED, that the International Reading Association support the efforts of parents to participate in determining the availability of reading materials used to instruct their own children, but be it further

RESOLVED, that the International Reading Association oppose policies which exclude from all students the availability of material for use in reading instruction.

Adopted by the Delegates Assembly
May 1980

IRA Officers at Time of Adoption

Roger Farr, President
Olive S. Niles, Vice President
Kenneth S. Goodman, Vice President-elect
Ralph C. Staiger, Executive Director

Board of Directors
Mary Ann Baird
Addie Stabler Mitchell
Jean E. Robertson
Norma Dick
Eleanor M. Ladd
John C. Manning
Nicholas P. Criscuolo
Bernice E. Cullinan
Patricia S. Koppman